MAKE YOUR OWN SUNSHINE

ALSO BY JANICE DEAN

MAKE YOUR OWN SUNSHINE

INSPIRING STORIES OF PEOPLE
WHO FIND LIGHT IN DARK TIMES

JANICE DEAN

HARPER

An Imprint of HarperCollins*Publishers*

HarperCollins books may be purchased for educational, business, or sales promotional use. For information, please email the Special Markets Department at SPsales@harpercollins.com.

FIRST EDITION

Designed by Kyle O'Brien

Library of Congress Cataloging-in-Publication Data has been applied for.

ISBN 978-0-06-302795-4

21 22 23 24 25   LSC   10 9 8 7 6 5 4 3 2 1

To those who shine their light so brightly on others

Kindness is the sunshine in which virtue grows.

—Robert Green Ingersoll

CONTENTS

MAKE YOUR OWN SUNSHINE

PROLOGUE

I had been planning myself an epic fiftieth-birthday party for a year. "Save the date" emails were sent out months before with fancy hotel rooms booked at the Bellagio, concert plans, spa reservations, and a big blowout dinner in the hotel restaurant's private dining room. Never in my life had I planned a crazy birthday trip like this, but you only turn fifty once. I figured this might be my only chance to do it up big. I bought a sparkly Vegas birthday dress that was fabulously flashy but comfortable enough to dance the night away.

And then, just a few months before my half-a-century birthday was to take place, a once-in-a-century pandemic helped bring everyone's big plans to a screeching halt.

My wonderful husband, Sean, thought if I couldn't go to Vegas, he would bring Vegas to me. He organized a special social-distancing fiftieth birthday for me during the pandemic by turning our dining and living room into a casino. While I slept, he spent the evening putting up a huge Las Vegas backdrop and setting up a roulette game on the dining room table. There were oversize playing cards and decorations all over the walls. He was in contact with my girlfriends Karen and Allison from Houston, who arranged for balloons and flowers to be delivered and set up in front of my house. They'd been on the invite list to help me celebrate my big five-oh in Vegas.

After a birthday breakfast in my Vegas kitchen, my friend Jillian Mele arranged a Zoom phone call with my coworkers from Fox. I took a screenshot of the *Brady Bunch* boxes with everyone who joined in to wish me a happy birthday via video. My sister-in-law popped by to bring gourmet donuts, a designer mask for me to wear, and even more balloons to add to the celebration.

Just when I thought things couldn't get any better, my husband told our kids to take me into the backyard and keep me there until four p.m. The boys had smiles on their faces but were sworn to secrecy. When it was time, I was brought out onto my front stoop while my oldest son, Matthew, grabbed my cell phone and started videotaping. I started hearing horns and fire-truck sirens. A parade of vehicles with neighbors and friends was coming down my street, yelling and singing "Happy Birthday" out of their windows and sunroofs. My little town's volunteer fire truck and a neighborhood police car were following Sean, who was dressed in a dinosaur costume (I love dinosaurs) and riding his bike while Matthew videotaped me with tears streaming down my face, laughing and crying at the same time.

My neighbor Dervla had set up a table in front of my house with champagne (for those who weren't driving). And even though I couldn't physically hug everyone, I felt those embraces from six feet away.

That day was so full of sunshine, despite the actual overcast skies and even darker circumstances we were living under. I told Sean afterward that the celebration of *five full decades* on earth during a pandemic was easily the best birthday I'd ever had. Vegas will always be there, but the day I had was something priceless that you couldn't buy. My expression in the video says it all.

My birthday celebration was just one of millions happening across the world for the months we were all in lockdown. Car parades were just one of the ways people were adapting to the new normal. These kinds of stories were happening everywhere. The huge cheers and banging of pots and pans that you heard every night, also featured on all the nighttime newscasts, originating from apartment buildings at seven p.m. to salute our heath care workers as they changed shifts. The opera singers on balconies, serenading audiences of next-door neighbors instead of the opera halls they usually performed in with thousands of people.

You heard and read about strangers using their stimulus checks to help businesses that were struggling to stay open, and restaurants that were donating meals to those who couldn't afford to feed their families. These real-life moments were sweeping the nation and being shared by millions through social media. We found out in this pandemic that kindness is also contagious.

I've been reading and writing good-news stories for many years now, and I thought I had seen my share of spreading sunshine. Then COVID-19 struck as I was halfway through writing this book. Incredibly, I started to notice *more* stories than ever before about the kindness and goodwill of others. During the most challenging times—and the darkest of moments—the goodness of others shines the brightest. You'll read about people in this book like Rebecca Mehra from Washington State, who early on (before we really knew the scope of how bad the pandemic would be) bought groceries for an elderly couple in a store parking lot who were too afraid to go in to get items themselves. There's Robertino the respiratory therapist, who decided to attach a picture of himself smiling to his PPE so that his patients would know what he looked like underneath his head-to-toe medical scrubs and mask; and there's the school principal who decided to go door-to-door to congratulate each of his students who couldn't have a proper graduation thanks to the lockdown.

My family needed bright spots, because in March and April we tragically lost both of my husband's parents to coronavirus. Along with thousands of other families, we experienced death without being able to see our loved ones before they died, unable to have funerals or celebrate their lives in the traditional ways we normally do to help with the grieving process. However, as we look back at these months of pain, we also see the moments of incredible kindness and sunshine that helped us get through it. I found that writing this book, and sharing the stories I was working on with my family, brought joy and comfort during these unprecedented times. Complete strangers became instant friends during the interviews, and I would feel so happy having that human connection, even if it was just virtually through an online teleconference.

My son Matthew and I would go for walks in our neighborhood, and I would tell him about my book on the kindness of others. He couldn't wait to find out about the newest interviews I had completed and the incredible real-life stories I was learning about. I told him it's a great lesson to be able to find and look for these moments of sunshine and allow the bright light from others to shine through.

We can be so powerful as humans when we are kind to each other. And it doesn't have to be big things—it can just be little moments between two people, like the story of the FedEx driver who took a few minutes to wipe down a package in hopes of protecting an immune-compromised customer. Kindness can cause a chain reaction toward others, like the man who sends roses to people who have lost their loved ones on Valentine's Day. From that chain reaction, a spark so powerful can begin a movement that spreads into communities or even across the world. There's the story of my friend Ray, a 9/11 firefighter who made sure his fellow first responders would be taken care of after being diagnosed with World Trade Center illnesses. But no matter how big or small, all of it is important. Sometimes we just have to look around for that light to hold on to.

Finding those moments is what I call "making your own sunshine." And the light from others will always help guide our way.

Even during the darkest days, one small gesture of goodness can lighten any mood or atmosphere. And sometimes it takes only a few seconds to make sunshine and pass it on. The forecast always needs a little more kindness and love. Here in your hands is a book filled with hope and happiness, but sometimes, as in life, that happiness and sunshine has to come after the stormiest moments.

Because I've learned one thing—as long as we have love and kindness, there will be sunshine, too.

Chapter 1

HANDLE WITH CARE

Social media can be a very dark place. Scrolling through Facebook or Twitter can make you feel pretty awful if you let it. However, it can be a tremendous place to amplify the good-news stories, too. Briefly, the pettiness gives way to something wonderful.

Carrie Blasi decided to share a story on Twitter that happened to her family during the pandemic. A FedEx delivery driver took an extra few minutes to sanitize a box before leaving it on her doorstep because he saw a sign saying someone at their house was immunocompromised.

Justin Bradshaw was the FedEx driver who delivered the box to their home in Boca Raton, Florida, and not only wiped down the box but left a kind note that said: "I sanitized your box when I saw the note on your door. Stay safe."

Carrie also had video proof from her home security camera capturing this kind act, which she posted. Thousands of accounts shared it, adding messages of hope and love. I was so grateful to talk to Carrie about the moment and why she wanted to put it out there for the world to see. I knew, as soon as I met her over FaceTime, that I instantly loved her and her family.

She says she never expected the story to take off like it did. It was the first tweet she had ever sent, and she did it to find the FedEx driver and thank him.

Emma, her youngest child, was diagnosed with type 1 diabetes when she was two and a half years old. Carrie is always thinking about Emma, now eleven. Especially now, with a virus known to hit diabetics hard. A lot goes into taking care of someone with this severe version of diabetes. Carrie and her husband, Andy, have been fighting it with Emma for nine years now, trying to keep her healthy. They constantly have to monitor her glucose levels. Their main concern is if Carrie or her husband were to get sick, who would care for Emma? None of the other family members know how to manage a type 1 diabetic, or give insulin, or change her insulin pump.

Carrie says she and her husband always manage everything for Emma when it comes to her health, and they're very up-front with her. "We let her know what will happen if she gets too much or too little insulin, and we've never had her change her own insulin infusion sites."

Because of the pandemic, Carrie is trying to teach Emma how to care for herself in case she or her husband gets sick. That's scary for caretakers who have a child depending so heavily on them. The details of what she and her husband do are incredible: "We have to check her blood glucose every three hours, and she wears an insulin pump that looks like a little beeper. It has a catheter that goes into her stomach or wherever I decide to put it. That gets changed every two days. She also wears a continuous glucose monitor on her arm that gets changed every seven days."

Carrie explains there's a wire that goes into Emma's arm, and it reads her glucose levels through her fluids. Those also all have to be changed. "So, that's seven days, and the insulin pump is every two days. But we have to dose her for every time she eats something, so you have to enter in the amount of carbs she's eating, you have to make sure her glucose levels are within her target range . . ."

Every day is different for Emma with her glucose levels. If they give her too much insulin and she drops too low, she could die. It's scary for Carrie to think that if she or her husband gets sick, no one else is capable to take over. Emma has had to go to the hospital only once since being diagnosed: Her pump was giving her too much insulin, and it was malfunctioning. It's a complicated and scary disease for a loved one to live and deal with.

I ask how they found out Emma had the illness. Carrie says at the time, they didn't know that much about it, even though they should have, because Carrie's paternal grandfather had it. "I knew he was diabetic, because he lost his leg. But I didn't know my father had it until we had Emma."

Carrie's father passed away before she was born. They never found out why he died.

"He was a basketball coach at a high school, and he was playing with a bunch of his friends when he collapsed. He started to vomit, and they didn't let him vomit—they instead started giving him mouth-to-mouth. So the cause of death was aspiration. But this whole mystery— why he passed out first. Why did that happen? We thought maybe he had an aneurysm."

After Emma was diagnosed, Carrie says she decided to find out more about why her father died. She kept thinking that maybe he also had type 1 diabetes and no one knew. Emma's endocrinologist went through their family history and asked if she could get ahold of Carrie's father's death certificate or autopsy report. They found it, and the doctor could tell right away from some of the levels on the report that Carrie's dad was an undiagnosed type 1 diabetic.

"The vomiting was a sign of diabetic ketoacidosis. Had they taken him to the hospital, they would have checked his glucose, and they would have seen that his blood sugar was extremely elevated, and he would have been a diagnosed. Back then, in 1969, they didn't go to the doctors if you were healthy. They didn't do family history checks and have all those warning signs. So, long story short, I should have known about type 1, but I didn't."

Carrie says they owe it to a neighbor, whose son was type 1, who helped her realize her own daughter had the same thing. She started seeing signs to look for. "At two years old, Emma was drinking a lot of milk, going through a gallon of milk every two days. When she would sleep at night, she would go to the bathroom through her diaper, and it would leak onto the floor. It was sticky, like syrup."

Carrie called her friend, who told her she thought Emma might have diabetes; she was thirsty and losing weight. Her friend told Carrie to take her to the doctor and have them check her glucose.

Carrie says type 1 is misdiagnosed quite a bit because the symptoms mimic the flu or an illness. "Sometimes doctors will check these kids, and they'll say, 'Oh, just let them sleep it off, they have a cold or a flu. Don't worry about it.' And send them home. And then these kids go into a diabetic coma."

When Emma's doctor said the same thing—she's fine, don't worry—Carrie told him to take her glucose. She didn't care if they charged her out of pocket. She demanded it. The doctor came back and admitted Carrie was right. "Normal glucose level is about eighty to a hundred. Hers was over seven hundred."

Emma was sent straight to the hospital, and she stayed over a week. Carrie and her husband had to learn so many things to keep their daughter alive. "I felt like I was back at school again. We had to learn all the things that we could and couldn't do with her insulin needs. That was scary; it's all she's ever known."

Carrie says if she could pick any kid to have something, Emma would be the one, because she handles her situation so well. "She doesn't complain. She doesn't cry. She doesn't fight me on anything. She's a good soul. And she's made it easy for us to manage her, but [like] any parent, I would love for her not to have this."

I tell Carrie how glad I am to hear her explain this illness, because I think as a society, unless you have someone in your life who has diabetes, not many people know how to diagnose it or what to look for.

And Carrie says she's so glad the kindhearted FedEx delivery man story gave her a platform, because not only is it highlighting the goodness from people in a pandemic, it's also educating people on type 1 diabetes.

"Because when Emma is at school, kids will say, 'Oh, you're diabetic because you ate all that junk food,' or just stuff that they probably hear at home. It's so heartbreaking for me to hear her come home and say that. And she's good, she brushes it off because she knows the truth, and she can either choose to educate them or not. But I'm glad that this is at least putting type 1 diabetes out there. So people will research it and read about it and know the difference between type 1 and type 2 diabetes."

It's not reversible, she tells me. It's not easily managed. "People don't understand that. If we don't check her, she could die. I hear about type 1s that go to college, and they go to bed, they're out partying, and they never wake up, and that scares me."

Carrie tells me that every time they get a package on their doorstep, a motion detector lets them know something is there to be picked up. At the start of the lockdown, she would go outside to spray the delivery with bleach. She'd then leave the box out until nighttime, when she could put gloves on and open it outside. She would then dump the contents into a basket and sanitize the contents of the package.

"So when I went outside to spray this particular box, I looked down at it and noticed there was writing on it that said: 'I saw your note, I sanitized your box. Be safe.' And then I looked at the box, and the label was all smeared, and I could tell that he was telling the truth. He had really sanitized it."

Carrie turned around and went inside and told her husband. "I said, 'Andy, you're not going to believe what's outside.' And of course, my husband is like, 'Oh my gosh, what's out there?' [chuckle] I'm like, 'He sanitized the box.' And he's looking at me like I'm insane . . . Because I get excited about this kind of stuff. And he said, 'That's great, Carrie. Awesome.' And Emma's looking at me like, 'When's dinner gonna be ready?'" [chuckle]

Afterward, her husband told her she should tweet about it. Carrie had never really used Twitter before, but she did, and she decided to also tag the local news channel in the hope that they might pick it up. "Because I wanted to thank him, because that was one of the nicest things, I know it's just sanitizing a box, but it was so heartfelt, and he did it out of the kindness of his own heart . . ."

Carrie also went back and watched the video on her security camera. "He didn't know he was on the video. You can see him clearly. He walked up to the box, took a step back, read the note, and then he thought about it. He made the decision to turn around and go get sanitizing wipes from his truck to wipe it down . . ."

Carrie tells me the note she leaves for deliveries says: "Somebody lives here that has an autoimmune disease. Leave the box. I'm not going to sign it. I'm not signing for anything."

Carrie says the note she posted never said to sanitize the boxes. That's why this delivery person was different. Many don't even take the time to read her warning. She laughs when she remembers one delivery: "I had a different person ring my doorbell profusely, because he needed me to come out and sign for a package, and I thought to myself, Do you not read?" [chuckle]

Meanwhile, the local news channel emailed Carrie after she posted her tweet and said they saw her story, could they run a piece on it? The next day she had a message from one of the FedEx driver's friends, asking if they could connect Carrie with Justin, the kind man who went out of his way to help sanitize the package.

"And, of course, they are amazing humans. Both he and his wife."

Justin's wife told Carrie she was grateful her husband was getting the recognition he deserves, even though he's really shy.

Carrie says Justin's daughter was born a micropreemie, so tiny that she could fit in his palm. That's one of the reasons why he took the extra step to help her sanitize the package. He would want someone to do the same for his family.

Carrie says they are amazing people, and she considers them part of her family now. Lifelong friends. She just knows it. "I would pick them as a friend any day of the week."

Carrie says when she finally spoke to Justin, he said he wrote on the box only because he felt that he had smeared the label so badly when he wiped it down. "He didn't want me to think he had ruined the box on purpose. I didn't really care about that. It was just the kindness, that he just . . . some people don't do that, they don't think to do that . . ."

Carrie says since the story went viral, she could spend days and days reading all the comments. She hasn't read one negative thing and realizes now more than ever that we need to hear stories like this.

"I keep thinking of that song 'Imagine' by John Lennon. If one person did what he did and just followed suit, I just can't imagine. We would be in such a better place as a country . . ."

I tell Carrie one of the themes I've learned from doing these stories is you have to look for the sunshine, or sometimes you have to make your own. Facing hardships is the most ordinary thing in the world. Most of us come to realize that the sunshine comes out after the storm.

Kindness is a skill, and it can grow from challenges that you've been through. Your life is precious, and every day is a gift, even the hard ones.

Carrie says now, when Justin drives by their house, he'll honk, and the kids will all know it was him driving by.

"What he did for my family is just one little thing, and I'm just one little person, but this story has given a platform to acknowledge kindness, and that kindness does matter. And do it, don't be afraid to do it."

I tell her there are so many layers to this story—the fact that it's educating people about type 1 diabetes, and also the FedEx company knows now that they have an awesome employee!

Before we end our call, I ask Carrie if things are getting better with a diabetes diagnosis. Is the technology is getting better? Is there hope on the horizon for those who have it? Carrie admits that she's given up on a cure for it. But type 1 diabetes, thankfully, isn't as scary for us as it used to be.

Carrie says for the first night ever, she and her husband had a full night's sleep thanks to the new insulin pump that Emma now wears. They still wake up and look at the monitor to see what Emma's glucose level is, but they don't physically have to get up and go into her room to check on her. Emma's new pump will automatically dose for high glucose trends and suspend for low glucose levels. As technology gets better, managing type 1 diabetes will become less scary.

"It's less finger pricking, too, because it shows up on our phone. I can see what her glucose number is, and I can see it when she's at school. So if I see she's going too high or too low, I can text her teachers or I can call the nurse and say, 'Emma is going too high, she needs insulin. Could you bring her into the clinic?' Or, 'She's too low, she needs juice.' So it's baby steps . . ."

I tell Carrie I'm also glad that she was an advocate for her daughter's health. I tell her I think this is a good lesson, that we have to speak up for our kids. If we as parents feel that something isn't right, our gut instinct can tell us a lot.

Carrie says she's glad she's had this opportunity, even if it took a pandemic and a kind FedEx man to bring awareness to Emma's condition. If it saves one life, then all of it was worth it.

Chapter 2

NAPKIN NOTES DAD

Most parents find packing lunches a boring chore. It doesn't have to be.

Because I work early mornings, I don't get to see my boys during the week when they wake up.

My husband, Sean, is the one who makes them breakfast, fixes their lunches when they go to school, and drops them at the bus stop. For many years, I expressed to mom friends how much I missed this part of their lives. My friend Karen suggested I should put little notes in their lunches. She did it with both of their kids, and even though it's a simple thing, she could tell they liked seeing the handwritten message. I loved this advice, and I decided to share jokes, which my husband puts into their lunchboxes every day. Not only did it make me feel good doing it for them, but they seemed to enjoy it as well. It's something that lets them know I'm thinking about them.

Since this little thing was such a hit with my kids, I decided to take pictures of the notes with jokes and post them on my social media. I've had many moms and dads ask me if they can use them to pass along to their children. That gives me great joy—knowing that my lunchbox-joke love is being spread to others.

When I heard there was another lunchbox dad out there, I knew he had to be a chapter in this book.

Garth Callaghan is known as the Napkin Notes Dad. He began writing notes to his daughter, Emma Callaghan, when she was in kindergarten. At the beginning, he made the notes simple, because she was just learning to read. Sometimes he drew pictures.

He did it as a daily source of inspiration.

He did it later on as something she would remember him for.

Garth was diagnosed with kidney cancer eight years ago. After the surgery, everything was fine; the doctors said they got it all and sent him on his way. Thankfully, though, one of his doctors realized that since he was only forty-two years old at the time, they should probably keep looking for the cancer. A year later, there was a different cancer, and not long after that, the original cancer metastasized.

Garth tells me he's been a metastatic kidney cancer patient for seven years now. "Which is kind of like the danger zone."

I ask how Garth is feeling now.

"This side of the grass is a good day. That being said, my gosh, I look at how I feel in a couple of different ways. Mentally, physically, spiritually, emotionally. All of those different aspects."

Physically, he says, it's tough. He's been in continuous treatment now for six years, and he's fatigued. His body aches. But his current treatment is much better than the first set of treatments, especially when it comes to fewer side effects. However, it impacts everything he does.

"I never was the first person in my family to sit down and say, 'I'm tired. I need to rest.' I was always the guy who woke up first. I was the person who went to bed last. And unfortunately, that's just not how my life is anymore."

I ask him when he started writing the napkin notes. What the inspiration was. He says the goal has always been to encourage his daughter in a simple, meaningful way. At the beginning, he admits he wasn't good at it. He was sporadic, and there wasn't a note every day. Sometimes he would add a piece of candy or cookie with the note. One morning, when Emma was in second or third grade, he forgot to write one.

"She came into the kitchen and scooped up her lunch bag and was walking away. And as she walked away, she opened up the bag, saw that there was no note in the lunch and turned on her heel, came back over to me, and held up the lunch bag almost like a Charles Dickens play and said, 'Napkin!'"

That was it, says Garth. That was the day it mattered. "I figured at that point that the notes really meant something to her. And if they meant something to her, they'd better mean something to me."

Emma was in sixth grade when her dad was diagnosed with cancer. He spent Christmas vacation recovering. After Emma went back to school in the new year, Garth says that the note writing felt a little different. "I wasn't sure what or why they were different, but I felt I definitely had a sense of my mortality at that point."

A week later, Garth says he caught Emma ripping up a napkin. "I thought to myself, Oh, gosh, how bad was that note? Was I off my game that day?"

He walked up to her and asked what was going on. She looked up and showed him that she wasn't ripping up what he'd written. She was ripping off what he had written; she was saving them in a composition book. She was concerned about his health.

"She wanted to save a piece of me in case I died. I looked at that composition book, and that's kind of where things shifted for me. I realized that these notes really meant something deeper for her."

After that, Garth started stockpiling his notes. He wrote hundreds of them in advance, so that Emma would still have napkin notes in case he passed away.

I decide to share my lunchbox-jokes story with Garth. Teachers will tell me how Theodore, my youngest, sometimes reads his out loud to the other kids. For a short period of time, Matthew, my eleven-year-old, didn't seem as interested in the jokes, and I asked him one day, "Do you still want Mama's notes? Do you still want jokes?"

He said, "I do. But, you know, put it in this little pocket here . . ."

And then there was a time when Matthew decided he was too old for the jokes. I was heartbroken when he gave me the sad news that he didn't want my jokes anymore, but I kept writing them for Theodore.

About a week goes by, and one day Matthew comes home and says he wants the jokes back in his lunchbox because his friends miss reading them. That made my heart sing.

Now, there have been a couple of times I have forgotten to write the jokes, and I start to sweat and feel like I committed a mom crime. I FORGOT TO WRITE THE JOKE! It's a terrible feeling. I tell Garth now I try to write two weeks' worth of jokes in one sitting, and then I put it on my calendar as a reminder: TIME TO WRITE MORE JOKES.

Garth laughs in agreement and says he's listening to my story, and his face hurts so much because he's smiling the whole time I'm talking about the lunchbox jokes. He says he thinks he knows the secret to our notes to our kids.

"We turn our kids over to schools for seven hours a day. And I've always been the working dad. So between work and Emma's doing school and sports and meetings, after-school activities, and God knows what else we have in our lives, I get to spend a grand total of sixty or ninety minutes a day with Emma."

That note we write, he says, means that for a few minutes in the morning, we're thinking about our kids and their day. And we're wishing goodness for them. We know that for just a minute in the middle of school, our kids will take a break and think of us. And our good wishes (or jokes) for them.

"It's that moment where I'm taking a minute to think about you," he says.

I ask Garth about some of his favorite notes he's written to Emma. I see many of them posted on his website, The Napkin Notes Dad.

Dear Emma,
 The moment you want to quit is the moment you need to keep pushing.

        Love, Dad

Dear Emma,
 Goals are reached only by moving ahead.

        Love, Dad

"There was a couple of years ago I wrote about one hundred and eighty notes. There's about one hundred and eighty school days. That year Emma started posting a few of them around the house."

Three of them, he says, got tacked up to the corkboard in their kitchen. One stayed on her dresser. Garth figures, out of the whole year, his score was five out of one hundred and eighty. "And you know what, from a certain point of view, that's darn good, right?"

Garth says the note that Emma kept on her dresser said something to the effect of: "Dear Emma, It only takes one person to really believe in you, even if that one person is just yourself." He says since then he's been trying to write notes that foster creativity, or a way to encourage a kind of persistence within Emma—to let her know to keep going no matter what life throws at her. "And some of the notes are just to let her know that I'm trying to foster those same qualities inside of me. Because let's face it. I know I've been fighting cancer now for eight years, and I need to let her know that I'm not going to give up."

Garth says if he ever creates a napkin notes company, the quote he'd use on the wall of his building would be from Mother Teresa: "If you can't feed a hundred people, feed just one."

I ask about his decision to write notes in advance just in case something happens and his cancer takes a turn for the worse.

"I did this after my third cancer diagnosis. My doctor started saying things to me like, 'The median life span for a patient like you is twelve months, sixteen with good treatment, and the five-year life expectancy is eight percent.'"

Through a long set of odd coincidences, Garth says he was sitting on a plane reading an article about a really cool guy, Alex Sheen, who is the executive of a nonprofit called Because I Said I Would. The sole purpose of the foundation is to help people make and keep difficult promises.

Garth says he put two and two together. "It was to have this inherent promise to Emma that I write notes to her every day." He didn't think he was going to be able to do it. "I was looking at the five-year life expectancy. Emma graduating high school in five years. This inherent promise to write notes. And I didn't think I was gonna make it."

But he sat down over the course of a few months and wrote out eight hundred and twenty-six notes, one for every school lunch day.

I ask where on earth he put all the napkin notes. He laughs.

"She's now a sophomore in college! Those eight hundred and twenty-six notes are still in the same box as where they were six years ago, because I've completely exceeded my doctor's expectations and my expectations, and I'm still alive!"

Garth says those notes have been set aside for safekeeping. And he didn't touch them. They're still there. He kept writing new notes every day despite having a treasure trove of notes to tap in to.

"Even now, in college, she has a note for every lunch day. And what I do for college is kind of like you, Janice, with your lunchbox jokes. I write them ahead of time. I look at the calendar and I think, Okay, it's going to be X number of days until I get to see her again, whether it's through breaks or weekend visits or whatnot. And then I write out enough notes to get her through that time. And she's learned some discipline there, because she doesn't want to read all of the notes all at once. She has to learn how to read only one a day."

I ask Garth about the positives of sharing this story of his. I told him when I was diagnosed with MS, one of the best things I ever did was going public with it. Even though I didn't want to be the poster girl for multiple sclerosis, if someone is newly diagnosed and I give them a bit of hope, then all of it is worth it.

He says, "It's really gratifying because I know that every time somebody wants to talk to me about my story, a couple of things can happen. One is I might be able to help somebody from a health perspective, whether they have cancer themselves. And they're trying to figure out how to better manage their treatment plan mentally as well as physically. Or I might help a parent write a note to their child."

I ask about positivity and if that sunny outlook helps a life span. Does he believe in that? For me personally, I find that because I was diagnosed with multiple sclerosis over fifteen years ago, I believe it has given me a much sunnier outlook than I had beforehand. And I think MS has helped me be a better person, a better parent, a better sister, wife, and mom. I think that a diagnosis of something health related does help in a desire to live a better life, or to have a better quality of life. Because it puts you in touch with your mortality and prioritizes things in a much bigger way than ever before.

"I wholeheartedly agree. I think one of the big challenges that I had in the beginning is that death kind of seemed to be always around the corner. And that is something that's really challenging mentally to get through. But I've always considered myself to be a positive person. I generally look at the bright side of life, and I've always been the type of person who kind of says, 'Oh, yeah, I can do that!'"

Garth says one of his mottoes in life is "What's the worst that can happen?"

"I mean, at this point, I've been diagnosed with cancer seven times. Right? So, if I try to do something that is remarkable or even a little bit crazy, what's the worst that could happen? Nobody is going to come to my house and knock down my mailbox or anything like that."

He says he lives by the notion of: You're going to get to the same place regardless, but you can choose *how* to get there in terms of your attitude. Like when it comes to going in for his cancer treatment: "I can go there as a grump, or I can choose to get there and walk the path of joy. You're going to end up in the same place. And the difference is how much are you going to try to enjoy the journey?"

I ask about Emma, if she carries that sunny outlook, like her dad. He thinks she does. "Think about how a child is impacted when their parent is diagnosed with a chronic illness. Back in the beginning, it was a pretty grave situation."

He remembers writing a note to her early on in his cancer diagnosis that said: "Remember that guy who gave up? Well, neither does anybody else."

He tried really hard to put a positive spin on everything he could. Even cancer. And now that Emma is a sophomore in college, Garth says he tries to stress that even though college looks like fun, it's a whole lot of work, too. Every morning when she wakes up, he wants her to think about three things she is going to be grateful for that day. And then be sure she's grateful for those things she thought about.

"In fact, this last batch of notes that I wrote to her, I had to write out about thirty days' worth of notes, and I made sure that at least once a week, that was on the napkin. And it said: 'Here are the three things I'm going to be grateful for today.' And then I drew three lines so she could fill in the blanks."

I tell Garth that's what my family does every night at the dinner table: talk about what we are grateful for. It can be simple, like: "Today I ate pizza at lunch." Or: "Today I was grateful the sun was shining." For me, I am just grateful for family. I tell him about the gratitude journal I try to write in on a regular basis as well. It helps refocus what's important. I then ask what Garth is grateful for today. At this moment.

I hear the smile in his voice as he remembers something and says: "You know, Janice, just yesterday—this is awful—I hate to rake leaves. It's like one of the chores that I loathe the most. And we have a property where there's a jillion trees in the back. I spent about five hours raking yesterday. My dog, Charlie, hung outside with me, and we were able to enjoy that moment. And look, if I were to be really honest, and I know this is going to sound a little corny, but I'm really thankful to be able to share my story with you. It's so easy for everybody to kind of get caught up in their day-to-day lives. The minutiae that we have, you know, between work, laundry, clearing the leaves, mowing the lawn, and vacuuming."

He says it's sometimes difficult to step outside of that life and look at the bigger picture—to quiet yourself and be thankful for what you have going on.

I tell Garth I feel grateful I was able to talk to him and, with all that's going on in the world, to feel a kindred spirit. Not only from the perspective of someone who shares a chronic illness, and trying to always look at the sunny side of life, but also the love of writing notes to our kids. That's something to be celebrated.

And then I remember one of Garth's notes to Emma:

Dear Emma,

Life goes by too quickly to leave important words unsaid.

- I love you
- I believe in you
- I know you are AWESOME
- Don't ever be afraid to be yourself

Love, Dad

AMEN.

Chapter 2½

EMMA THE NAPKIN NOTE KID

I was so touched after I spoke with Garth, the Napkin Notes Dad. I kept thinking about his thoughtful responses after we talked. About how powerful his message was, and his beautiful relationship with his daughter, Emma. I often wonder what goes through my boys' minds when they get a little lunchbox joke from me. Does it affect them the same way it does me? Feeling like I'm part of their day despite physically being away from them? If a moment of kindness can be profound, what about years?

I decided I wanted to hear from Emma herself. We arranged a phone call and spoke during the pandemic as she was finishing up her sophomore year while at home. Emma is studying American politics and law at Washington and Lee University.

I start off by telling her what an impact her dad's conversation had on me, and that, after hearing how much her father truly loves his daughter, I felt I had to get her voice in the book as well.

I ask her first to tell me about her dad and what he means to her.

"My dad is my favorite person in the world. He has always been really close to me. When I was growing up, I spent unimaginable amounts of time either following my dad around, hanging out with him while he did work, or . . . I can remember one time when we were just bored in the house on a weekend, and we set up this mini–golf course all throughout my entire house."

She says they've always done stuff like that together. Even though their relationship has changed as she's gotten older, they still have fun. But now he serves as a friend and adviser as well. "He's always available to give advice or talk to me or anything like that."

I ask her if she can recall the first napkin note he wrote.

"I can't even remember when it started. I know it was when I was in kindergarten, and I was really young, because for me, they've literally always been there."

Like Garth told me, Emma says the notes evolved over time. "They used to be just very short stuff, and as I got older, they became more in-depth, and detailed, and more emotional. Sometimes harder to read. But I can remember third grade was the first time where I had a difficult day ahead of me, with a hard test or something where I was worried, and I can remember having a note that really calmed me. They used to be just fun little things. And then, as I got older, they evolved into more relevant topics."

Emma says even though she's in college, her dad still writes notes. She'll read them when she's having her morning coffee. The ones that make her laugh the most are those that have cursing involved. "He'll just write: 'Get shit done,' or something like that. That makes me laugh the hardest."

Emma says she can't imagine that Garth is able to find any more quotes. He's been writing them for so many years. Now the ones that hit home for her are the notes written from his heart. "Even things just like: 'I know you have a hard test today, you got it.' Or sometimes he'll sprinkle in a little note that says, 'Call me.' Just a reminder for us to stay in touch while I'm in class."

Emma's school is two hours from home, and before the pandemic, she says, her dad would drop off a box of notes after his cancer treatments. The treatment center is an hour away from her, and he goes once a month. I ask how her father is feeling.

"He's doing well. I think he is better suited to be home than the rest of us, because he's always worked from home, or at least for the past few years he has, so that's not a big change for him. The infusions are getting harder with time, but it's only a few days at a time that he feels bad."

Emma tells me her dad is looking forward to his final treatment for a while. Once you have the full course of medicine, it's supposed to last the rest of your life. I tell Emma how amazing this news is. Especially since her father originally started writing the notes to her because he thought he might not live to see her grow up.

"It's absolutely a blessing. I mean . . . I don't know, we've been forced to think about his mortality so many times, and just with every rediagnosis, it's hard to trust that it really might be his last infusion, but it's also an incredible thing to hope for."

I ask Emma if she thinks her father's hope and optimism, sunny outlook, and love of life helped him overcome cancer in some way. She agrees and says when he was first diagnosed, she was in middle school, and Garth talked to her about how hard it was at first. The news that he might not live more than five years was, of course, shocking. She saw him withdraw and be quieter. It was hard to see him like that. Seeing him in pain physically and emotionally.

But he was able to turn the darkness back into light somehow, finding his stride and learning how to deal with the setbacks. Emma says it didn't take long after the original diagnosis to get it back. He became happier. Perhaps even happier than he was before the cancer.

"He would take walks with us, encouraged us to eat healthier, and helped make dinner, and tried to be around people. And I think even if it didn't directly impact his health, it definitely impacted his happiness and ours, too, because he was able to hang out with us more."

I ask Emma, when she reads the notes from her dad, what goes through her mind?

"When I was younger, I always got asked in interviews if it was embarrassing to always have a note from my parents, because I guess a lot of kids would have that sort of little worry or embarrassment. But I guess because it was always a thing for me and my friends. They knew my dad and loved my dad. He played with all of us growing up, and it was something I shared. We were all excited to look at whatever he had drawn or written for me for that day."

Now, she says, the notes and their meanings have changed for her. She says it's a way for her to ground herself. She incorporates reading what her dad wrote every day. It reminds her that even though she's at college and her parents aren't with her, she can always reach out and talk to them every day. "It's a reminder that they're there, they're thinking about me."

Emma laughs and says the only issue now is the storage problem for all the notes. "At school, I kept them in a shoebox. But now I've been in school for two years. I've got just this stack of shoeboxes at home that I keep them all in, but I also have all of my apartment stuff from school at home. And it's just . . . we don't know where to keep them anymore!"

I ask Emma to tell me about her mom. What's she like?

"My mom and my dad are very similar in some ways and very different in others. My dad is the type of person that will get close to someone after a long time, and likes to build a few really strong relationships, and of course he's nice to the strangers he meets. But my mom is a lot more social than he is. She's very warm and willing to talk to anybody about anything. She really is the glue that brings us all together. She's a very caring person."

Emma tells me one of her favorite stories about her mom. Her best friend's mother was diagnosed with breast cancer and didn't want any help. This is a common trait that cancer patients have when they first learn they have it. They don't want to be a burden to anyone and feel like they can battle it alone. The friend's mom refused to pack a lunch for herself because she was going through chemo and she wouldn't be hungry.

"But my mom, almost every day, would go out and find something that she knew she would like to eat, and would bring it to wherever she was. She was working at a retirement home and my mom would go bring her a Subway sandwich. My best friend would tell me: 'My mom hates to admit it, but she loves the food your mom brings her.' And she just . . . she takes care of people. My mom is the best caretaker I know."

Emma tells me her mother was one of the biggest supporters of her dad when he started getting asked to do interviews about his napkin notes. "We had a lot of chats about this when I was younger, but it was just so strange because my dad, who we see as a more introverted kind of figure, all of a sudden, everybody's taking this moment in our daily lives and poring all over it. They're interviewing him and interviewing us, and it's all a little weird. Like, what's going on?"

But during that time, her mom was supportive of everything. The first interview they had as a family, Emma's mother packed up everything they needed for an overnight trip to New York. "She really snapped into action, and has been a supportive figure for all of it, and been very helpful with, I think, connecting us to the people that really need to hear the story."

I ask Emma if she would do the same for her kids someday. Would she write notes to them, too?

"Absolutely. Yeah. I mean, it's one of those things that's adaptable to any situation, no matter what. I think it's something that you can change and fit into what they need to hear even if they're not reading yet. If I'm sending them off to preschool, then I can just draw a little doodle of our family or something like that. It's just something to bring you closer together."

I tell Emma the same story I told her dad about how my Matthew, for a short period of time, told me he might be too old for the jokes and wanted to take a break, but then about a week later decided I could put them back into his lunchbox because his fifth-grade friends were asking where his mom's jokes were. I was so grateful.

Emma says she understands how Matthew was feeling at the time. "It's always funny, because it's something that you don't feel like you need. And when you're a kid, all you want is to assert your independence and be like, 'I don't need to read notes.' And you don't need to, but it's always *nice* to."

I ask Emma, with all that's going on with technology, are we losing something with our human connection? She thinks we can do both. "My family is very technology-dependent. My dad loves all the new stuff. I think we find ways to make the technology work that aren't alienating to a person-to-person connection. In many ways, it works out that we are able to use it to connect even more."

I tell her there might be something to that. I feel like even though I do love talking to people face-to-face and physically sitting down to write a note to someone, a nice text that pops up on your phone can also help turn things around. Even if it's "Thinking of you today."

I ask: What advice would you have for parents who want to connect with their kids again? She says there are always different things you can do, depending on the age group.

"I think finding a way to get family time, no matter what's going on in your life, is essential. I've always been a very busy person with sports, I played softball my whole life. And then in high school, I was on the debate team and the Model UN team. And so basically every weekend, I was somewhere else, and every weeknight, I had softball practice or a game or something like that."

At least one parent was always there to see her play or be at important school events. She felt loved and supported. And family dinners are a must. Emma says it's absolutely necessary to have set times when you are together. Spontaneous family moments can be important.

"My parents will come up now and say, 'Hey, Emma, we're going for a walk after dinner. Do you want to come?' Just having those things that you can do to remind yourself that family is not a chore, and it's something that you can have fun with and have lifelong connections through."

I end our conversation by asking Emma what she's grateful for.

"I am grateful for a lot of things. One of the things that my dad always does whenever I'm sad or stressed out is he tells me to just take a break and write down what I'm grateful for. So that list always starts off with my parents, how they're always there, they're always supportive, my friends, the things that I have that keep me alive. And then I stray on to things like my cup of coffee in the morning, and my napkin notes, and the fact that I'm going to go get pie with my best friend tonight. So, it's always, I don't know . . . For me, and I think for my dad, too, it's finding the little things. To always be grateful for the big things, but to enjoy every little thing that you come across."

I tell Emma about something I've been doing with my son Matthew lately, since the pandemic. We've all been spending a great deal of time with our families, and it's the most time I've had with them since maternity leave. Every other day I will go for a walk or a bike ride with one of my kids. And Matthew loves to hear about the stories I'm working on for this book. I was so happy to tell him the story about Garth, the Napkin Notes Dad, and how even though his daughter is in college, he still writes notes for her. I tell Emma I'm connecting with my boys by telling them about these real-life moments that are happening every day with families and strangers.

Together, Matthew and I started to see how many of these stories there might be and how much the world needs them right now.

Chapter 3

MS JOURNEYS

Many of you know that I was diagnosed with multiple sclerosis over fifteen years ago.

My first major flare-up happened in 2005. I woke up one morning and literally could not get out of bed. I had numbness and tingling in my feet and thighs. I was so exhausted, it was difficult for me to even move.

The first doctor I saw told me my symptoms could be anything from a slipped disc to multiple sclerosis. She told me I needed to see a neurologist and get an MRI. Neurologists use MRI scans for examining the brain and spinal cord.

My MRI showed lesions on my brain and spine. I also had a spinal tap that showed I had proteins in my spinal fluid, which further confirmed my diagnosis.

According to the National Multiple Sclerosis Society, multiple sclerosis is a chronic, unpredictable disease of the central nervous system, which is made up of the brain, spinal cord, and optic nerves. It is thought to be an immune-mediated disorder, in which the body's own immune system incorrectly attacks healthy tissue in the central nervous system.

There's no way to predict how a person's MS will progress. I have relapsing-remitting MS, which means my attacks or exacerbations subside with full or partial recovery. Others have a more aggressive type of the disease that causes a steady progression of disability from the onset of symptoms, with few or no relapses or remissions. And there are others who are somewhere in between.

There is no cure for MS. However, there are more than a dozen medications that have been shown to modify the course of the disease, reducing the number of relapses and delaying the progression of disability to some degree.

When I was first diagnosed, I began researching and reading as much as I could on MS while trying to remain optimistic. I found wonderful people along my journey who offered me hope and encouragement and helped me make my own sunshine in a time of darkness.

I also found people to talk to who were living with MS, people who were not just functioning but thriving. There are many moments of great struggle when it comes to dealing with a chronic illness, but I do take great solace in those who don't let their challenges prevent them from doing bigger things with their lives.

While researching this book, I found people who were living with the same illness I am and were doing incredible things. For this chapter, I wanted to introduce you to a couple of amazing women who won't let their illness limit their dreams.

Janelle Boston was diagnosed with MS in her twenties; for many years, she said, she was fortunate, and the illness didn't interfere with her life too much. She got married, had two children, and had a job at a bank in Tully, Australia. It never got in the way of her happiness, and for many years, she even held back on telling her two boys that she had the disease. She didn't want them to worry.

More recently, Janelle says her diagnosis got worse, going from relapsing-remitting to primary-progressive. In the beginning, when walking got tough, she would hold on to her husband and hope that no one thought she was drunk. But things got harder, and now, at the age of fifty-five, Janelle has lost the ability to walk. For the most part, she says, she's been lucky on this journey, and she's had the attitude of "That's life, and this is the hand I was dealt." She never had regrets, but there was one thing she wished she had done when she had the opportunity: climbing a mountain.

When Janelle was a member of the Girl Guides, there was a trip to Mount Tyson, one of the most beautiful landmarks in Australia. The hike was called off due to bad weather. It was something Janelle thought about a lot over the years.

In February 2019, when a Tully Facebook community group chat asked people to post things they had always wanted to do but never had the chance, Janelle felt compelled to put her wish out into the universe, even though she never thought it was possible. She wrote: "Climb Mt. Tyson . . . when I was in the Girl Guides we were going to climb it but the weather turned bad so we didn't do it."

Graham Sollitt, the administrator on the website, replied: "Never say can't or never, there's always hope."

After inquiring how they might make Janelle's wish come true, the Tully Rugby League said they would gladly take on the challenge. They called a fitness trainer, Tracee Harris, who, coincidentally, already worked with Janelle, to see if she could get involved and come up with a plan. Tracee put a message out on her Facebook page. Instantly, many of her clients responded, with other local athletes joining in.

Ms. Harris got in touch with a local welder who helped design and build a special chair to help carry Janelle up the mountain. She would be carried by dozens of people who wanted to help her get to the top of the mountain. The trip took five hours.

I ask Janelle if she was ever scared, going up the mountain with all these strangers carrying her.

She says she never was. "It was such a happy environment. You could see everyone was excited to do this for me." And, she says, she was "feeling the love."

Janelle tells me when they were climbing the mountain, it was cloudy, and once they got to the top, the sun came out. "It became so clear, you could see all the islands. They were eighty miles away from us."

Janelle talks about how wonderful everyone was, and adds that a few members of the team checked her legs to see if there was any swelling from the special chair she was in for five hours. Just a simple act of kindness about how her legs were doing is something she'll never forget, on top of this extraordinary mission.

I ask Janelle's husband Jim how he felt that day. He joined in "huffing and puffing behind her," he jokes. "Oh, I was emotional. I had a tear in the eye. I couldn't hold it back when I got to the top. It meant so much to her."

When I ask Janelle if she has any advice for those newly diagnosed with MS, she says she feels bad for those who are dealing with any kind of illness, but she hopes they stay strong for as long as possible. She's learned that clean living, looking after yourself, and respecting your body helps in doing the right thing.

I ask if the illness makes her appreciate things more. She says she's naturally an appreciative person and tries to look at everything like it's a blessing.

She then adds: Things right now aren't looking as good for her.

Her husband, Jim, tells me she now has increased activity in her brain from her last MRI.

I tell her I'm sorry. And she says, "What can you do? You just have to deal with it."

But she has a great support system, children and grandchildren she wants to see grow up.

Before we hang up, Jim tells me that his wife and I have many things in common: "You have the same birthday. And two boys."

"And a loving husband," I add.

As we say goodbye, I remember what I read about Janelle when she was climbing that mountain with the help of all those new friends: "She just smiled the whole way—couldn't get the smile off her face."

That kind of smile takes teamwork.

CHERYL HILE IS another woman who wouldn't let multiple sclerosis keep her from her goals. She was diagnosed with MS in 2006.

Cheryl began running six years before her diagnosis. She loved that it was an activity she and her husband, Brian, could do together, and it filled her with joy.

"It's the endorphins. Exercise is very important for me because I want to continue to be as healthy as possible. I like long-distance running because there's just something about the endured exercise that just makes me feel really good. I feel accomplished afterwards. It gives me that calmness to get through the day."

It also helps her connect with Brian. "You don't necessarily have to talk while we're running, but just having him by my side and seeing his footsteps out of the corner of my eye—it's kind of this nice rhythmic pattern. We live near the coast [in California], and even just hearing the waves . . . it's a stress reliever."

After Cheryl was diagnosed with MS, her first neurologist advised her to lower her expectations. That upset her. She wanted to prove that doctor wrong. Instead of feeling sorry for herself, she found a way to continue her dream—and then some.

"But there has been a decline mentally, cognitively, as well as fatigue. And I have a lot more weaknesses."

Cheryl says she's now going through disease progression. At forty-six she notices that she doesn't have the energy she used to, even for simple tasks, like writing an email: "It takes me forever because I have to keep going back, rewriting my sentences because they don't make sense. Everything just takes longer. And my doctor is saying I have probably dipped into secondary progressive MS, where the disability from living with the illness gets steadily worse."

Cheryl says initially she got depressed after her diagnosis. "I didn't know anybody with MS except for my coworker. And she was in a scooter. She had trouble getting around. So I thought, Well, you know, that's my future. And I'm eventually going to be in a wheelchair, use a cane, whatever."

She went on antidepressants, but her husband encouraged her to keep running and exercising. She registered for several races because she didn't know how long she'd be able to run before the disease took over and made it impossible.

The tripping and falling started in 2007. She thought she had a sports injury. She ran the New York City Marathon and almost fell a dozen times. "I had to run practically with my hands in front of me, just to brace myself. If I tripped, I had to catch my fall."

Cheryl started doing research and found out that dropped foot (experiencing difficulty lifting the front part of the foot) is a common symptom of MS. That was the point when her neurologist told her to lower her expectations. And that's when she decided not to give up. "No way, I'm not going to lower my expectations. I'm going to prove her wrong. I'm going to keep on running."

Cheryl was able to find a podiatrist who referred her to a clinic that specializes in outfitting people with prosthetics and orthotics. She went through different brace designs until she found one that worked for her.

Once she was fitted with it, she started setting goals. Striving for something helped her push forward with the disease. It began with signing up for races and marathons. Running all over the world, she was able to meet people who had the same goals. And she felt like she was back in the driver's seat. "I want to be the one to decide I don't want to run marathons anymore, rather than the disease dictating when I have to stop."

I ask Cheryl her what she tells people who are newly diagnosed. She says having MS isn't a death sentence. You can still have a great life. "You're probably going to have to work a little bit harder at it than most people. But you'll be ok as long as you have that positive attitude and set some goals, and find your passion."

She says it doesn't mean you have to run seven races on seven continents, but even if it's just small things and making efforts to work toward those moments, whatever they are, find something that's doable and enjoyable so you keep on doing it.

Cheryl says you can make your own sunshine by doing something for yourself that makes you happy. And by doing that, you might inspire others around you without even realizing.

I ask if having MS makes her appreciate life more—and focus on what's important in life.

Cheryl says she wouldn't be talking to me now if she didn't have MS and we didn't find each other. And she's had opportunities running races to meet wonderful people who support her and also those who share the same illness.

She adds: "I think that the both of us are making the most of it. We're not taking the backseat and letting MS drive our lives. We're in the front seat of our own car and trying to do something. Having a positive impact, not just for ourselves, but being good examples for other people and helping other people."

Cheryl, thank you for going the distance for all of us who live with MS.

Chapter 4

FRIENDLY SKIES

I've heard about incredible acts of kindness at airports and in airplanes over the years. I'm not sure what it is with traveling. So many stress traps come with heading to the airport: packing, getting to the airport, timing the traffic, checking bags, waiting in security lines, and hoping that your flight is on time. Short tempers and frustrated strangers are just a few steps away. But there are also incredible, inspirational heartwarming acts of kindness, many of them made by strangers who are dealing with their own challenges in terminals and on the planes. My friend Bethany Mandel shared a story on Twitter of a kind stranger who helped her on one of the darkest days of her life.

"When my mother was dying, I flew home from Belgium, where I was living, to say goodbye. I was sixteen. I missed my connecting flight in DC. The next one wasn't until morning. It was the day after Christmas, and everything was all booked up. I called my mom's friend, and she told me she didn't think my mom would make it until I got home. I crawled under the phone booth and absolutely lost it. The folks at the gate—the passengers—pulled me out, and I barely got the story out through my sobs."

A passenger coming home from a business trip to spend a belated Christmas with his family brought Bethany up to the gate and switched flights with her so she could be on the next plane an hour later. She says she thinks about it all the time.

"The guy had already spent Christmas away from his family and signed up to sleep on an airport floor so I could fly home. It was so generous. And everyone was from Rochester, New York, and thus fighting over who got to give me their seat. It was incredible. Random women holding me as I waited for my flight. It was a magical moment in a really dark place."

How do you get to be that person? How do you become a person who steps in to help others?

One of my favorite stories of kindness happened in an airport a few years ago; I remember reading it online and bursting into tears. Perhaps it's because I'm a mom and I can relate to traveling with small kids. It's a very simple story: A mother is trying to get her child onto the plane. Her kid has a complete and total meltdown and will not move from the terminal floor, where he's kicking and screaming. She can't get him to listen. Within minutes, a little group of women who don't know each other gather to help the mother and her son get on the plane. Even though I read it a few years ago, it has always stuck with me as one of the most memorable stories I've ever heard. I often reference it when talking about random acts of kindness. One of the women who helped that day wrote a post on Facebook about it. It was shared hundreds of thousands of times. I got to talk to Beth Bornstein Dunnington, the woman who came to the rescue.

Beth lives in Hawaii. She's originally from New York but has been living on the Big Island for many years now. She's a writer and teaches writers' workshops. One of her goals is to empower women to find joy in their lives.

I tell her I love that she's someone who looks on the sunny side of life. I can identify with that. She believes it comes from within, and it's through life experiences that she tries to always find joy. It's in her personality that she is always on the lookout for sunshine. Part of the reason why is that she is a cancer survivor. She found out about her diagnosis in a nontraditional way.

"I was walking down the street, and I had an epiphany—some might call it a spiritual experience, or a religious experience, or a guardian angel on my shoulder. Suddenly, I felt like something was wrong. I knew where it was in my body, but I had no symptoms whatsoever."

Beth comes from a family of doctors. She's the only one who isn't in the field of medicine. She found a doctor, and instead of letting him examine her, she demanded a CT scan immediately. The doctor gave her a hard time and made her pay for the test out of pocket. "They thought I was crazy. But as it turned out, my instinct was right, and I had lung cancer but with no symptoms!"

She then traveled to Boston, where her father was affiliated with Mass General Hospital. She remembers lying on the table and asking the head of pulmonology why she didn't have any symptoms and how she knew and felt that there was something wrong.

He told her it wasn't her time to leave this earth. That she'd had a realization. Because by the time lung cancer spreads, it's in your brain, it's in your bones. A few years after that, Beth met a hospice worker who explained that there's a term for what she'd experienced: It's called the Knowing.

Beth says since then, she's learned she isn't alone in having this happen to her. Sometimes people have an epiphany or a realization about something going on in their body with no explanation.

"And the reason I'm telling you my cancer story is because after that, I said, 'You know what? I lived, I obviously need to pay attention to that, and I need to up my game in terms of what I bring to the planet.'"

Beth says she feels like the good-news stories are the ones that hold her interest now. And that's why she "pays attention." So when she found herself at the airport, she decided she was going to be the person who got up to help. "Because my eyes are open, and I'm looking around for it."

Beth says she was on a workshop tour, heading to Portland from LAX, and she remembers there were three gates for three different flights taking off from there. "I was sitting there, and there was a young kid, like around eighteen months old, having a meltdown. So, we're parents, we know what that's like. The mother was pregnant, and she was traveling alone. The kid was just kicking, lying on his back. Screaming, then running around, and she couldn't catch him. Everybody was sitting there and watching. It was one of those situations where your heart goes out because you're like, 'Oh my, she's pregnant—and it was a situation where it was hard to pick him up. The mother's head went down like she was about to give up. She started crying while her child was melting down."

Beth noticed a lot of people in the terminal, but the ones who got up to help were all women. And no one prompted anyone to help. "I don't know who got up first, but we stood up and gathered around them. They were on the ground, and we all helped. I sang to the boy. I think I sang 'Itsy Bitsy Spider' because that's what I used to sing to my kids to calm them down."

Beth says someone had a piece of fruit and an unopened bottle of water. The mom drank the water. Then a toy appeared, a little dangly thing, and they were able to distract the kid. He started to come out of his tantrum.

"It was just . . . a beautiful moment. We never introduced ourselves to each other, nobody felt the need to even say anything. You know, 'Let's take a picture . . . What's your name? Where do you come from? Where are you going? Are we on the same flight? Are you on her flight?'"

Beth says after that, the mom and her child got on the plane. It was just a few minutes, but it made a big impact on her. She decided to write about it and post the story on Facebook. At first she didn't make it public, but her friend wanted to share it, and it went viral from there. I asked her if the mom ever reached out or if someone tried to contact her. Beth said after the thousands of comments and shares, no one came forward. And in a way, she's glad, because it was meant to be an anonymous experience. "It was just, 'Here's what happened.' We didn't take a picture or exchange information. It was just a beautiful moment."

I tell her that's why I love what she did so much. Because it remained kind of a quiet story even though it was shared millions of times. There were no selfies or photo shoots afterward. It was a paragraph that, in the grand scheme of things, meant so much more.

I ask Beth if she's always been that type of helper in life.

"I think I've always been that way. I think that's just my personality. I grew up in a home that was filled with a lot of joy, music playing, all of us singing, and knowing that in a moment, we can have joy. And help someone."

I tell Beth it's one of my all-time favorite stories. I thank her for sharing it again for all of us.

Not everyone can lead a movement to change the world, but everyone can find a way to help someone else, just a little, just for a few moments.

One more story about flying home. This one involves a brand new family traveling together for the first time.

Dustin Moore decided to write about his experience on a flight home with his wife, Caren, and their newly adopted baby girl, Mackenzie.

He wrote: "It's been a difficult week. But rather than publicly air my grievances, I'd like to share with you the kindness strangers offered us the day we brought our daughter home. I hope our story uplifts you, and reminds you there is goodness to be had in this world."

Mackenzie was just eight days old, and they were traveling with her for the first time after having just met her. Caren was thinking of all the things that might go wrong on the flight. She tried to recall all the information friends and family had given her before the trip. "You're always worried when you see a baby on a flight, going, 'Oh no, I hope that they're not crying the whole time.' We had no idea, especially with an infant, with takeoff and landing, the pressure changes in her ears, when do we feed her?"

Dustin decided he wanted to sit at the back of the plane in case there were any disruptions or spontaneous crying. "We were trying to keep a low profile; we just wanted to be on the flight and get home. [chuckle] Nothing else. Mackenzie fell asleep, and about midway, she woke up and was fussing. I instantly wanted to get her changed and taken care of. So I got ahold of one flight attendant named Jenny, and I asked her if there was a space in the back for us to get her changed."

Jenny said she would help set something up. Dustin then got up to change the baby. He noticed Jenny with another passenger near the line for the bathroom. "And then they both said, 'Oh, your daughter's so beautiful. If you don't mind us asking, why are you traveling with such a young baby?'"

Dustin told the story of the adoption and how they were bringing her home. "Five minutes later, another flight attendant, Bobby, comes up, and he squats in our aisle, and he says, 'So, I heard you guys had some exciting news to share.'"

Dustin and Caren introduced little Mackenzie to Bobby and thanked him for his kindness.

A few minutes after that, Bobby was on the intercom of the airplane: "Ladies and gentlemen, there's a very special guest on the flight today. She's only eight days old, and she's traveling home with her mom and dad!"

Dustin says as soon as Bobby finished his announcement, everybody in the cabin started cheering and applauding and whooping and hollering. That's what made the experience so emotional for him: the excitement from complete strangers. He and his wife were feeling overwhelmed and insecure, and for them, this moment was everything.

After that, napkins and pens were passed around to all of the passengers so that they could give their advice and well wishes. Dustin says the most amazing thing about that was there were sixty-seven people on the flight, and every single person wrote a note of congratulations or a small bit of advice, except the five people who were asleep.

One napkin read: "I was adopted 64 years ago. Thank you for giving this child a loving family to be part of. Us adopted kids need a little extra love. Congratulations."

Every time he thinks about it, Dustin says, it makes him tear up. "I want her to grow up and be proud of where she came from, be proud of her mother and father. Be proud of the fact that she had a chance and that she was raised by us, that we adopted her. And that will be something that she carries with her for the rest of her life."

On his Twitter feed describing that day, Dustin wrote:

What all of those perfect strangers and attendants did not know was the emotionally tender state of two brand-new parents. Parents who after so many years of trying had been blessed with their first child. Parents who felt scared but determined in their new role.

The Moore family adopted Mackenzie through an agency. They were at the hospital in Colorado when their birth mother delivered.

The adoption process was stressful and worrying, which made the celebration on the plane even more meaningful.

Although this story sounds picture-perfect, the journey wasn't so easy. Dustin and Caren tell me that they had been trying to have a child for nine years. They had tried every procedure under the sun. Medications, IUI (intrauterine insemination), IVF (in vitro fertilization), and there were pregnancies but many miscarriages, including multiple sets of twins. There was always excitement, anticipation, and then the heartbreak of heartbeats that never made it.

Caren says it was incredibly tough on them. For so many years. "One after another pregnancy and trying to hope for the best. 'Okay, this is it, this is it.' Or: 'They found out what's wrong. Okay, this time, let's try this.' And even at the end, our fifth round, we did immunotherapy with it, where it's half the doctors say, 'Yes, there's something to it,' and the other half are saying, 'No, not so much.' But we figured, 'You know what? We'll try it.' And so, well, that was the most extensive, where it was additional thousands of dollars of testing, and we had a nurse come to our home and do the bag with an IV for a couple hours."

Caren was feeling both angry and sad that she couldn't get pregnant. There had been so many feelings and letdowns. "It was a struggle, especially after our last loss, of pure and utter defeat on my end—as a woman in that department, thinking, Okay, I wish I could conceive or maintain a pregnancy, and, Why isn't my body working? and, Why don't they know why this isn't happening and why nothing's sticking, so to speak, with that?"

Caren says they went through a period of thinking maybe they just were not meant to have kids. Maybe that was their journey, and they would just have to be thankful for nieces and nephews. Both of them love kids so much. Having children is all Caren has ever wanted.

"Since I was twelve, I wanted to grow up, I wanted to get married and have my own family. It was my dream. And struggle after struggle, pregnancy loss after pregnancy loss, it was just hit after hit after hit. And we're both good with kids, and we love kids. And we have friends with little kids, and they're always all over Dustin. He's playing. He's meant to be a dad."

After all of this, they began talking about adoption. Dustin says they went all in. The certification in California took a few months. After that, there were a few ways to go about it. You had to first find a child who needed a home, and there were multiple channels you could look into. There were companies whose business was basically like a broker where they match families wanting to adopt and expectant birth moms, or children who are in need of a home. The Moore's found a service that gave them a year's subscription for free. Shortly after that, they were reached by a birth mom.

"She was in her first trimester at the time, when she reached out to us, with our daughter. And we kept in close contact with her. This was something that we definitely learned along the way, that we would tell anybody, is that if you have an opportunity to, you should develop a good relationship with the birth mom."

Once they found the birth mom, she was very honest with them. It was between Dustin and Caren and another couple. They communicated via texts and emails. Then they contacted each other through video chats. They planned to meet in person and made the trip to Colorado. Dustin says it felt a bit like a blind date.

They were corresponding back and forth. Carrie says it was strange trying to get to know each other and share very vulnerable, private parts of their life when not a lot of people are open to sharing things. But they were going to go for it. Be open and honest. Lay everything out with all their cards on the table. They were given the news that the birth mother had chosen them to be her daughter's parents.

I ask Dustin and Caren about opening up their heart to kindness. "This moment of joy on the airplane that was shared with the world—is that part of opening your heart to sunshine?"

Caren says it was. The emotions were sometimes overwhelming, especially on that plane ride home, "with everything we've gone through the last nine years to finally get to that point. And what Dustin said, worrying about is everyone going to treat our daughter the same? Are they going to show love and support? Because she's adopted, instead of her biologically coming from us. And that's why it meant so much more to us, I feel like, is because of everything we'd gone through. They had no idea. They had no idea of the struggle we were going through or how long we'd been going through it."

I say you never know what someone's journey is, and the best thing is just to be kind. I tell them about the interview I had with Beth (the helper mom at the airport). It restores your faith in humanity. Caren agrees: "It does. And that's exactly what happened with us also. Because in the airport, before we were going into security, there was another couple there. We must have looked like newbies, because they're like, 'Okay. What are you doing?' I asked, 'Do I take her out? Do I hold her? Do I keep her in her car seat? How does this go?' They said, 'Oh, no. You need to take her out, and you hold her this way. And put your car seat on there this way, because they're going to have to flip it . . .' It was everything. They were really helpful with that."

Dustin tells me a few other details about when Mackenzie was born that really brought home to him that this was meant to be. When they were looking for a place to stay in Colorado for an indefinite period of time, waiting for Mackenzie to be born, they asked their church to see if anyone knew of places or people who could help. A couple who were members at the church said they had a place for them to stay.

"Total strangers opened up their home, which, for them, big risk. Because it was like, what if they were weird, or what if we were weird or something like that? It was like, no problem. Just the sweetest people."

I ask Dustin, when he looks back on his tweet and how it went viral, what was his mindset when he posted it? He confesses to me that at the time, he was thinking about something that bothered him at work, in particular someone who had done something dumb, and he felt an urge to share it online. And then he picked up his daughter, Mackenzie, and decided there was enough of that kind of narrative out there. Why not instead put out something uplifting?

"I thought, You know, let's put something good out there instead. And I thought about the story from the flight home with our baby and thought, It seems like a perfect chance to share that."

He posted his good-news tweet on a Saturday night, and the next morning, thousands were sharing it.

I tell Carrie and Dustin about how I try my best to keep my tweets "mostly sunny" as well. People tell me that's why they follow me, because Twitter can be such a dark place. It's nice when there are the bright sunny spots. They stick out. Dustin agrees and says he loves telling this story to people because it brings them joy and it inspires others. He says people tell him they've decided to try and adopt, too. And they are talking about adopting again.

Dustin adds: "It's beyond my ability to express how much it means to us, and we're very happy that it's been able to do something uplifting for other people, too."

Sometimes, on the journey of life, you can choose to walk on the sunny side of the street. And that in turn may lead you to a life filled with more joy and clarity.

Chapter 5

FATHER-DAUGHTER DANCE

For my birthday one year, my brother Craig gave me one of the greatest gifts of all time. He made a video of me with old pictures my mom gave him at the age of five, doing a reading of *Alice in Wonderland* in my basement. There was an old cassette tape of the reading that my mom had kept over the years. He was able to transfer it and use it as a soundtrack to my childhood. As soon as I opened it up, it was like time travel, because in the background of my five-year-old self reading, you could hear the voice of my father. I hadn't heard his voice in many years. It was very brief—after me yelling, "Daddy, I think it stopped! Can you come help?" he said, "I'll be down in a moment." And then I heard him coming down the stairs to help me stop the big 1970s tape recorder and begin the recording again.

I hadn't heard my dad's voice in close to twenty years. He died un-expectedly several years ago, and we hadn't spoken in a long time. Our relationship was complicated, but when I was a little girl, he was my hero. When I opened up that special video my brother made for me, I was instantly brought back to those beautiful moments in my Raggedy

Ann pajamas with my hair in pigtails, reading a story and knowing that my dad was close by if I needed him.

When I stumbled on the story about the bride whose wedding dance involved an audio recording of her late father, I felt compelled to interview her and the brothers who thought of this incredible gift.

On September 22, 2018, Kaley West Young was celebrating the happiest day of her life in her home state of Utah. She was getting married, and her whole family was there to celebrate. The one person missing was her beloved father, David. He passed away of heart disease three years earlier.

Kaley's brother Kevin had the idea that all the brothers should take turns dancing with their sister to honor their father who wasn't there. "It's every girl's dream to dance with her father," her brother announced at the wedding reception. "Obviously, she can't do that, but as brothers, we have the opportunity, and we'd like to dance with her for her father-daughter dance."

The song "Fathers and Daughters" by Michael Bolton began playing, and Kaley started dancing with her brother Kasey. Just a few moments into the song, a familiar voice came over the speakers: "Hi Kaley! My name is Dave West, and I'm Kaley's dad, and I love her very much. Eighteen hundred times' worth."

As you watch the video, it's hard to describe Kaley's reaction. I gasped when I saw it online; she was understandably overwhelmed with emotion. She told me she was struggling to stand. "I was trying to keep myself composed, but honestly, the only thing that I felt was complete love."

Her brothers had decided that, to make the moment special, they would play the song in its entirety, with short clips of their dad's voice taken from home videos and voice recordings.

Kevin explains how it went down: "About six months prior to the wedding, my wife and I were throwing out ideas, trying to collaborate to see how we could include my dad somehow into the wedding. We decided to do a dance with Kaley, with all the brothers. There are five brothers, and then there's her. She's the youngest, and the definition of daddy's girl. And it just progressed from there."

Kevin's wife was the one that thought of putting their father somehow between the lyrics. He was someone who loved home movies and leaving voicemails, so there was plenty of material to search through. Kasey West began putting it together months before by watching videos and grabbing the sound bites, and it took off from there.

The reaction from the guests in the video was emotional, too, but I wanted Kaley to describe it herself: "You could feel it. I don't think there was a dry eye in the room. Everyone that knew my dad was crying and our family. And then my husband's family, who didn't know my father, were also crying just as much."

She says you could feel the love her dad had for them. He always talked about how excited he was to walk his daughter down the aisle one day and have that traditional father-daughter dance. "I knew in that moment that he was there. We could feel his presence around us."

Kaley's brother Dustin West's role was to convince Kaley to go through with the dance to begin with. "She initially said she maybe didn't want to do it because Dad wasn't there. So, I tried to make her feel like it was still a good idea. And all the brothers were there for her instead . . ."

I ask Dustin if he heard the finished product before the wedding.

"Kevin had sent me a portion of the video, of the audio, but I had refrained actually from listening to the full song. I wanted to be surprised. I heard the first part, where he says, 'My name's David West. I'm Kaley's dad.' But the very end was the part that I hadn't heard. His send-off message. It was so incredible, and something I was so happy to be a part of."

Each brother took some time to dance with Kaley, one by one, before the song ended. They cried together as they danced. The room-ful of wedding guests stood silent, watching the beautiful moment in awe. Dustin says it was the perfect way to pay tribute to their father, a guy who loved everyone.

When they posted the video online, they thought only a few people would see it. Dustin was the one who found Michael Bolton on social media and tagged him with the video of the dance. Meanwhile, Kevin posted the video on Facebook for friends and family who weren't at the wedding to be able to watch. Within twenty-four hours, the viewers were in the thousands, with hundreds of comments.

And then *the* Michael Bolton shared it to all of his followers, writing:

I'm humbled and honored that the West brothers choose my song #FathersandDaughters to dance with their sister Kaley at her wedding. Their video brought me to tears.

He also thanked Kaley's brothers for choosing his song for the special tribute.

I ask Kaley and her brothers about the comments and stories shared by strangers who had seen the video. Kaley says it's a reminder to everyone who sees the video that family is most important. There's love in the world, and that's the greatest gift we can ever have, to share our story. The world deserves to see that love coming back.

At the very end of the song, once Kaley has danced with all of her brothers, their dad's voice comes on and says: "You know, I just want to let you know that I love you guys. And I'm really going to miss you."

They tell me they retrieved that message from a voicemail their dad had left for a family member who was moving away.

I ask how their mom is doing and what she thought of the idea as it was all coming together. Kevin was the one who told her about it. "We were actually heading up to a family cabin six months prior to the wedding, and my wife played her just the song. We told her what we were thinking of doing, and she broke down in tears and told us it was perfect."

It was a long process, sifting through hours and hours of videos and phone messages and finding the perfect clips. Kevin admits that "in the end, she was blown away. And even more so now with all the people it's brought joy to."

Kaley says her mom has been lost in the shadows a bit during all of this, but she's their number one support. "And everything that we say about our dad, that's her, too. They were a team our whole lives. So, this tribute was about our dad because he wasn't there, but our mom is here, and we love and appreciate her so much."

I ask the family if they still get messages about the video even now, two years later. Kaley says every single day. And many say the video brings them comfort. Some couples were inspired to do the same thing at their wedding.

Kevin says they receive messages from people who have lost contact for whatever reason with their parents or with their dad. "Our video made them want to reach back out to their parents. That part has been so inspiring for us."

A woman named Paula left a post saying she was a wedding photographer and had witnessed over a thousand wedding dances. "The love that this shows us is what Dave West instilled in all his children and especially Kaley. What a blessing to the West family, and now to all of us privileged to have it move us to joyous tears."

A father of four daughters said he watched the video and then shared it with all of them. "This has me crying buckets no matter how many times I have watched it, it is so beautiful how you incorporated your dad's voice into the song, wow, just WOW . . . Thank you."

And from a Vietnam-era U.S. Air Force vet: "I consider myself a fairly hardened man, but I have a daughter, too, and this video yanked my heart out. God bless those brothers for what they did for their sister."

This moment lives on in spite of Dave West's death. I ask Kaley to describe her dad and what she remembers most.

"He was a ball of joy. He had humor and love that affected all of us, and me in a way I would've never known without him passing."

She says she didn't realize until after his death the messages he was able to convey to his kids without even having to verbalize them. He lived his life for his family and the importance he put on his kids and making sure that they all got along and were there for each other, even if they were in the middle of a fight or a disagreement.

"We always had and have a respect and understanding for one another. That came from our parents and the love that our dad had and still has instilled from within."

Kevin says family is everything. "On my dad's headstone, it says: 'Friends come and go. But family is forever.' My dad would always say that to us."

I tell Kaley that I think her dad was put on this earth for a greater role than any of them realized.

Kevin is astounded at the number of people who have watched the wedding video. On all the platforms—Facebook, Twitter, Instagram—there have been 350 million views. And the comments that people leave are incredibly touching. The video changes people, and it's one of the most loving things the family has ever seen. Their dad is spreading love and joy even though he's not here.

Kaley adds that the biggest takeaway from this moment is to let everyone know that when you're going through hard things, whether it's a death, a grievance, a divorce, a loss, or any kind of hardship in your life, it's a reminder that you're not alone.

"And I'm lucky to have five brothers that have my back no matter what, a loving mom, and a dad who loved me—and is still showing his love all of these years later."

She says she realizes a lot of people feel alone right now, especially those who have lost a parent. She hopes that by watching her wedding dance video, it can be a reminder that we're all capable of getting through hard times. "I want it to be a reminder that you are never alone. Love transcends beyond the physical body, and whoever is going through a great loss, no matter what it may be, you are never alone, and you are loved."

At the end of our conversation, I thank Kaley and her brothers for sharing their story with me. There's a reason why more than three hundred million people have watched that video and have been touched by it. It's a simple story about a dad who, even though he couldn't be with his daughter on her wedding day, still had a presence that was larger than life.

I open up my own video that my brother sent to me with the voice of my dad filling my ears. I close my eyes and listen again. He's right there at the top of the stairs again. He remains in my heart and close by in my memories.

The end of the Michael Bolton song says: "Fathers and daughters never say goodbye . . ."

And at the end of my tape recording, my dad's voice is heard saying "Good night"—and I say "Good night" right before it ends.

Chapter 6

CUTS ABOVE THE REST

When I come across stories about people going the extra mile for others or going above and beyond the call of duty, I notice many of those who practice what they preach the most are teachers. We all remember the teachers who made a difference in our lives.

A good teacher can change how you look at the world, and a great teacher can change how you look at yourself. I wouldn't be the person I am today without the guidance of some of my teachers. They have helped map my success and shaped the person I am today. And they still help me develop as a parent and a human being.

A few years ago, my son's third-grade teacher, Mrs. Klein, gave me a gift to help tell both my boys that I had multiple sclerosis. One day Matthew came home and said his teacher was in a wheelchair because of a disease called MS. She talked to her students about it openly and honestly and told the class just because she can't walk doesn't mean she can't do what she loves to do. I took that moment as a door opening for me to have an honest discussion of how I have the same disease as Mrs. Klein, and like her, I wasn't going to let it stop me from being a good mom. I'll never forget that moment. I wrote about Mrs. Klein in my book *Mostly Sunny,* and when the book was published, Matthew brought it to her, and they took a picture together. It's one of my favorite photos of all time.

I still keep report cards and handwritten notes from teachers I've had. Some of them are yellowed and torn from decades ago, but I will never get rid of them.

So much of what we all need is a kind person to mentor us, a person who cares and is wise and willing to shepherd us through the confusing parts of life. When I read about wonderful teachers in the news, I want to share their stories with everyone. It may inspire others to become educators. More often than not, it's not about how they teach that gets our attention, but the way they interact with their students that makes the headlines.

Robert Dunham teaches fifth grade at George W. Carver Elementary School in Richmond, Virginia. On the day his school was hosting their "moving on" ceremony, a graduation ceremony from elementary to middle school, he had the inspiration to grab his hair clippers before he left the house, thinking they might come in handy.

Robert learned to cut hair from watching his father in his barbershop in Brooklyn, where he grew up. And over the years, in his spare time, he would watch videos on YouTube to help hone his skills in case he ever needed them again.

On graduation day, Mr. Dunham thought that some of his students might not be as prepared as they wanted to be. He says he woke up early, knowing it was an important day. As he was headed out the door, his wife stopped him: "Where you going with those clippers?"

He smiled and said, "Something tells me some of my students are going to need a trim."

Robert knew that something as simple as a haircut could give them a little boost of self-confidence on their big day.

When he offered the service to his pupils, to his delight, several students put their hands up. So, Mr. Dunham set up a makeshift barbershop in his classroom.

The word spread, and teachers down the hall were coming in, asking if they could add one more to the lineup of students needing a little trim. Ms. Randolph, who witnessed the action from fourth grade, took the picture that went viral.

Mr. Dunham says he never thought his free haircuts would cause such a reaction. He just wanted to make sure his students were looking their best. "Just being able to be that positive male role model for a lot of my students is just something I take pride in doing every single day." He says that his students are some of the "brightest and funniest kids on the planet."

Mr. Dunham knows that Carver Elementary wasn't always known for the free haircuts. A few years ago, a state investigation revealed a cheating ring led by a former school principal. But Mr. Dunham says don't judge his school by what's happened in the past.

A lot of his students come from places where they are dealing with a lot. Some of those challenges, he says, most adults wouldn't be able to handle. Mr. Dunham is one of those teachers who wants to be there for his students no matter what.

Over the years, he feels like he's become a surrogate dad, since a lot of them don't have father figures in their lives. His father was always there for him, so this is his way to pay it forward. "I'm always going to be there for them."

Mr. Dunham wants to leave his graduating students with a positive message: "Remember to always get caught doing the right thing, remain humble, and it's not always about how you start, but it's how you finish."

He says it's important for him to lead by example and show his students what doing the right thing looks like. "I always look at it like this: We all go through something even as adults. But it always seems to be that one person happens to come along that may not even know what you're going through, but they always come with that word of encouragement or all those random acts of kindness that literally say that, you know, I know you're going through something. I don't know what it is, but I want you to know it's going to be okay, and you keep doing what you're doing. That's the kind of teacher and person I've always strived to be every single day."

And having a good haircut can help. "I know when I leave the barbershop, I feel good. If you look good, you've got that confidence starting to come out of you." He wanted every one of his students to feel that sense of pride on their special day.

Mr. Dunham can't believe this one act of bringing his clippers to class would have so much impact. "I literally stopped for a minute to kind of, like, you know, gather my thoughts and emotions. Maybe after this, people can start finding ways to be nice to each other. That means I've done my job."

Once in a while a student will still come to Mr. Dunham and ask him for a haircut. Mr. Dunham always says yes, but with a deal in mind: "You got to get a least a B or an A on the next assignment!"

I mention to him that the act of cutting hair requires trust between the person cutting and the person receiving. He's giving them love. And an exchange of trust. It's a simple but very moving gesture, for a little boy who may be in need.

Like Mr. Dunham says, sometimes it takes only a haircut to make someone feel better. There's definitely sunshine and kindness in those beautiful clippers, and in the teacher who carries them in his briefcase.

A haircut isn't the only way a teacher can show every student they are worth feeling beautiful.

———

SHANNON GRIMM TOOK notice that her student, five-year-old Priscilla Perez at Meador Elementary School, was quieter and somewhat sad during her class. "Priscilla was a little shy when she first came to our classroom, and she had a hat on that she didn't want to take off. She took off her jacket, backpack, et cetera, but the hat stayed. I didn't push it. I wanted her to be comfortable. But it wasn't just one day. She kept it on for weeks and months. By and by, the kids starting to become curious, because they're in kindergarten."

The other kids started wondering and talking about why she needed her hat. They wanted to take peeks underneath. As it turned out, Priscilla was scared to take off her hat because she had short hair. The kids would try to pull her hat off, and she got so upset. Mrs. Grimm took her aside and asked her why she was so sad about her hair, and she admitted that the other kids thought she looked like a boy. Priscilla would come to class crying and say she didn't want to be in school anymore. That broke Mrs. Grimm's heart.

Priscilla didn't have any underlying health problems. She didn't have a crazy haircut. She just felt very different at an age when different can seem disastrous. Someone needed to show Priscilla that different can also mean special.

"As a teacher who values my relationship with my students far more than anything else in the classroom, I knew that this was important. I needed her to like school. Otherwise, she wasn't going to learn. She wasn't going to progress and be successful. So, I made sure that over Christmas break, I would figure something out."

Mrs. Grimm had an idea. Winter break was coming up, and the teacher was going to make an appointment at her neighborhood salon. "I was in bed one day, and I woke up in the morning, and I was like, 'I need to cut my hair!'"

When everyone got back after vacation, students were shocked to see that their teacher, Mrs. Grimm, had chopped off her long hair.

They also realized her haircut was very similar to that of their classmate Priscilla. Mrs. Grimm told her class: "I think I look beautiful. Don't you think I do, too?"

I asked Mrs. Grimm what Priscilla thought of her new haircut.

"It's like one of those videos on Facebook you see of a kid opening up a box and it's a puppy. They're crying because they're so happy. It was kind of the same emotion that she was showing. She was crying with this big smile on her face. It meant absolutely everything to me, because I knew at that moment something was different. It had changed. It had changed for her. It had changed for me."

Mrs. Grimm realized it wasn't just about Priscilla. It was also setting an example for the other kids in class. "It was about everybody else in that room and getting them to understand that we're going to accept everyone who walks in our life and that is around us and that we interact with—just because they look different, that doesn't mean they're any different than you or I."

Mrs. Grimm says it was one of the most rewarding moments in her teaching career.

Not only did Mrs. Grimm show off her new haircut, she bought dozens of matching bows that she and Priscilla could wear, too.

When Priscilla's mom picked her up that day, she got off the bus crying and said, "Mom, Ms. Grimm cut her hair. Just like me!"

In an interview with a local television station, Priscilla said, "I would cry because I would think the school was not fun. My mom cut my hair even though I wanted long hair."

Mrs. Grimm thinks teachers have to think about each child's situation. If they take the time to understand where a student is coming from and how he or she is being raised at home, then they can better understand how to help at school so that a child can be more successful. "Because they're not going to want to learn from a teacher who doesn't respect them."

Mrs. Grimm says the students know if their teacher cares or not. And they're going to be willing to try harder if they know their teacher is there for them. "I felt by cutting my hair, I was experiencing what Priscilla was going through. It's the same emotions." But perhaps, as a child, Priscilla didn't know how to process those emotions.

Mrs. Grimm says she was able to set an example at home with her own kids. Her son, who also was in kindergarten at the time, said, "Mom, you look like a boy. Why did you cut your hair?"

She used it as a teachable moment: "I said, 'Well, that's why I cut it. Because you and all my friends in my class think that short hair on a girl means that they're a boy, and am I a boy?'"

Her son said, "NO!"

She then asked: "Am I still your mommy? Even with short hair?'

He said yes.

Mrs. Grimm told her son that it doesn't matter if she has short hair or long hair. She's still going to be his mommy and will still be there for him, tucking him in at night. "That's kind of the way I talk to my students. Mrs. Grimm is still Mrs. Grimm. I haven't changed one bit because of my hair. Short or long . . . I'm still gonna give you hugs every morning when you come into the classroom. I'm still gonna give you a hug when you leave. I'm still a girl. I'm still going to teach you!"

Like a flower, Priscilla blossomed in school. Her confidence was restored, and she, along with the rest of her kindergarten class, learned an important lesson. Mrs. Grimm tells me that Priscilla said to her one day: "When I get big like you, I will have friends who will be mean to me, but I will be nice to them just like you." Mrs. Grimm says that moment, along with many others, made her smile and realize that she was so glad she became a teacher.

I told Mrs. Grimm that teachers are like sunshine. Learning from them can make you "brighter," too!

By the way, Priscilla, I just want you to know, if you're reading this or someone is reading this to you right now: My mom cut off all my hair when I was your age. I remember that day like it was yesterday. I have many pictures of me with my short hair. Stella, my mom, told me that it was the style back then. A famous figure skater named Dorothy Hamill had short hair, and my mom thought I would look good with the exact same hairdo. And even though my mom thought it looked pretty on me, *I did not.*

When I look back at pictures of me with that short Dorothy Hamill haircut, I realize I was still the exact same person. Short hair or long hair. But what I wished for back then was a friend like you, or a teacher like Mrs. Grimm, to help me feel that I was beautiful, too.

Chapter 7

BABY STEPS

When we are compassionate, we are acknowledging that we all share the same human experience. Being compassionate toward others can lead us to more acts of kindness. And they can be small things, for no reason: "just because" moments.

When kindness happens unexpectedly, it can be a game changer. Some people describe it as fate, happenstance, being in the right place at the right time. Whatever way you think of it, it can restore your faith in the world.

Sometimes you can change the course of someone's life, as well as your own, with the tiniest decision. Like this story about an Uber driver who found herself in the path of a new mom who needed a ride but needed a friend more.

Nikki Ihus flew from Kansas City to St. Petersburg Johns Hopkins All Children's Hospital to have her baby. Her boy, John Henry, had been given only a small chance of survival. The nurses mentioned to Nikki not to Google anything when she found out his diagnosis in utero.

John Henry was born with congenital diaphragmatic hernia (CDH), a rare defect where there is a hole in the diaphragm, which allows internal organs to enter the chest area and moves the heart over to the right side, keeping the lungs from developing.

Children's Mercy in Kansas City and the Mayo Clinic in Rochester, Minnesota, both said they could not do anything to save her little guy, so she joined some groups on Facebook to find out if there were options that gave her son a better chance at survival.

"I ended up contacting Dr. David Kays at Johns Hopkins Children's team in St. Petersburg, Florida, who is the best in the world when it comes to this condition. They got back to me fairly quickly. I sent them all of my medical records, all the tests we did."

Instead of a 5 percent chance of survival, they gave the baby an 80 percent chance. Nikki, her husband, and her mom decided to fly to Florida and have John Henry there.

He was immediately placed on machines to keep him alive. "His lungs didn't fully develop. And it was really important right after birth that he had that support. He was attached to a machine that helped his heart and lungs for almost thirty days. Then he was weaned to a ventilator, so that was still pretty much breathing for him. And now he is on a machine that people use at night to keep their lungs open."

Doctors told her John Henry would likely be in the NICU (neonatal intensive care unit) for at least four months. And Nikki was worried about not having any income after November, when her short-term disability ran out.

In a journal entry posted online, Nikki wrote:

John Henry is a part of a program called Beads of Courage. Essentially, he earns a bead for everything that he does or gets while he is in the hospital. For example, every night in the hospital is a bead and every day on ECMO [extracorporeal membrane oxygenation] is a bead. Needless to say, after 27 days of being in the hospital, John Henry's string is about 14 feet long! Well, today is a special day because it is the LAST DAY he has earned his ECMO bead.

That's right . . . John Henry has been taken off ECMO! He is oxygenating all of the air that is being put in his body by the ventilator and he is doing great. So well in fact that the doctors decided to remove his cannulas. They were planning on leaving them in overnight, but his numbers have been so good they are positive he will not need to go back on ECMO!

Nikki's mom and husband had to fly back to Kansas City for a little bit to take care of things at home. During those days without her little support group, Nikki was overwhelmed, scared, and homesick. Her son was doing well in some things, but there days when the complications made her worry.

To take her mind off what was going on at the hospital, she decided to call an Uber to take her to a children's consignment store to buy John Henry some baby clothes.

Belinda Smith was the driver who got the call. The destination was Johns Hopkins Children's Hospital, and the first thought that went through her mind was: I hope it's not a sick child.

Belinda pulled up and saw Nikki. She knew right away that Nikki was having a rough day. She asked how she was doing when she got in the car. It didn't take long for Nikki to open up. She started to cry.

Being a mom, it was hard for Belinda to imagine what Nikki was going through, but she realized that just being able to listen was something she could do. Nikki getting in that car, Belinda felt, was for more than just a ride.

I ask Nikki what made her decide to tell her story to a stranger when she got in the car.

"I was really having a horrible day. They had placed my son on his stomach for the first time, but he was still on life support. And he wasn't getting the results they were looking for. I hadn't really told anyone what was happening that day, and I'm usually someone who bottles up my feelings. I got into this Uber not thinking I was going to tell anybody what was happening. When Belinda asked how my day was going, I couldn't pretend. She seemed like a kind person, and I just opened up to her. I guess it's true what they say, it's sometimes easier to tell a stranger what's going on."

Belinda says she just tried her best to cheer Nikki up during the ride to the store. Once they arrived, she decided she couldn't just drop her off and leave her there alone. "So, I parked the car and I turned off Uber and I went in and found her looking for clothes in the zero-to-three-months section."

She put a hand on Nikki's shoulder and said: "This should be a really fun day for you. Let's shop."

Nikki started to feel better. Belinda wanted to do something more, so she sneaked over to the front of the store with the clothes she was holding for Nikki and told the salespeople she wanted to buy them all.

She gave the bag of baby clothes to Nikki with a note that said, "No pressure, but if you need anybody to talk to, here's my number." Then she gave her a hug.

Nikki was taken aback. "For this stranger to go completely out of her way—stop what she was doing, stop making money at her job, and to come be with me for a couple of hours to shop for the baby—that was just incredible."

Ultimately, this act of kindness was a bright spot in what was a dark time in the life of a new mother with a sick baby. Nikki admits it touched her heart in ways that are hard to describe. "She's my hero."

I ask Belinda what made her decide to go in and join Nikki inside the store.

She admits it was an instant decision. "I mean, I pretty much knew after I dropped her off that that's what I was going to do."

Nikki says the fact that Belinda wanted to buy the clothes was also incredibly thoughtful, and it was something that meant more than just a credit card transaction.

I ask her if she'd ever encountered kindness like this before, and she said that people have always asked how they could help. She said she never really accepted that help and always wanted to do things on her own. She didn't want to be a burden to anyone. However, it's hard when you have something this major going on.

I mention that sometimes when you open your heart a bit more to others helping, that's when it happens.

I ask Belinda if she's just one of those people who always has a sunny disposition. She says she tries to be. She decorates her Uber car for the holidays, gives out candy, too—whatever she can do on a short ride to help her customers feel good. She also practices what she preaches when it comes to her own day-to-day life.

"I try not to allow myself to get upset at the small stuff, like if someone cancels a ride or something doesn't work out because it's just not meant to be. And sometimes I pick up people that just need somebody to listen to them. No matter how big or small their problems may be, you never know what somebody is going through. You just have to be there and give them a smile or a friendly word and hope someone would do the same for your own self."

Belinda says she is a firm believer that only you have the power to make a situation different. If you feel that life is taking you down a path that you don't want to go down, you have to make a change.

"But sometimes, if somebody just gives you a little push in the right direction, then they lean in towards helping themselves a little more."

Nikki was so touched by what her new friend did for her that she posted a picture of John Henry in a onesie that Belinda bought for him that said "I'm a Superhero" on it. They are friends for life.

Still, not every story of helping others has a happy ending. After writing this chapter, I was visiting the website where Nikki was updating everyone about John Henry's health. My heart broke when I read her last entry:

March 9th, 2020

We have some sad news to share. Last week, the neurologist and Dr. Kays let us know that John Henry's brain damage is more extensive than originally thought. He will probably not be able to move his legs, learn how to eat by himself and will have severe cognitive slowness. In addition, his lungs still have not started to recover. So on Wednesday, March 11th, we will be discontinuing John Henry's care and letting him go.

Over the next couple of days, Joe and I will be spending precious time together with John Henry. So we ask that people don't individually message us with apologies. Please keep us in your thoughts and prayers. We love you all.

I considered leaving this story out of the book. But John Henry, like all of God's miracles, had a place in our world, and he deserves a place in our hearts. Even though he visited us for only a short while, his birth brought upon tremendous acts of kindness that deserve to be shared. His mom, Nikki, tells me she's glad this chapter is included because it will bring awareness to his condition and maybe help future parents and babies who have CDH. Perhaps it will make others feel comforted and not alone in their hardest moments, and it might encourage people to do wonderful things in memory of John Henry.

You never know what kinds of burdens other people are carrying. However, you also never know how easy it might be for you to lift a little bit of that weight off them for a while.

Chapter 8

SOMETIMES YOUR LAST CHANCE IS JUST THE BEGINNING

I believe having children is the reason I was put on this earth. It's hard to put into words the way I feel about my two boys other than they are two halves of my own heart, and they make me a better human being. I tear up when I think of them and what they mean to me. So, when I heard about Liz Smith, a woman who always wanted to be a mom and thought she might never be one until she met a tiny little girl with big blue eyes who needed a mommy, my heart grew a little bigger. After Liz told me her story, we agreed that fate had brought us together to share her story.

Liz Smith is the director of nursing at Franciscan Children's in Brighton, Massachusetts. She's been a nurse for twenty-four years and has had a wonderful, fulfilling career taking care of others. Even when she was a little girl watching her own mom, who was a nurse, she knew someday she would be one too. Her mom even framed a certificate from the Hasbro School of Nursing for her daughter.

Liz's career was going well, but there was something missing. She wanted a child and, as she describes it, kept looking for a husband to help her dream come true. The spouse never showed up, and she began to think motherhood wasn't in the cards. When Liz was in her forties and getting out of another failed relationship, her sister took her aside and told her she didn't need to find a husband to have a kid. She shouldn't lower her standards trying to make bad relationships work in order to start a family. Liz said she went into a deep depression because of it. "I never imagined becoming a mom would be a challenge," she said. "It's a desire you can try to push away and fill with other distractions, but it never goes away."

She was in tremendous pain. "I was a strong, independent woman, with a successful career, always on a positive trajectory, and I found myself really sad and depressed. And when I thought that door of being a mother had closed, I wasn't coping well."

Liz says her sister was very supportive and suggested going to a fertility specialist to try a sperm donor. This was something she never thought she would end up doing but went ahead and tried. After several months of fertility treatments, it wasn't working, and the insurance wasn't helping to cover any of it. She couldn't pay for it on her own, so Liz says she closed the door on the dream of being a mom. It devastated her.

When others asked if she was looking into adoption, Liz was stubborn, saying if she was meant to have a child, it would be biological. Her friends and family kept suggesting she look beyond the traditional way of having kids. Two weeks later, Gisele came into her life.

"I was coming out of the medical unit, and some of the staff were pushing this baby in the stroller. And she just she caught my eye, and I said, 'Oh my gosh, this is a beautiful little girl!' The staff introduced me to Gisele, and I know this sounds crazy, but I believed right away that she and I were going to be tethered somehow. I didn't know her backstory at that time, but I quickly found out after that she needed a medical foster home. So, that's how we met."

Liz had just started at Franciscan Children's and didn't know many people. No one knew her private struggle to become a mom and how sad she had been. All of a sudden, when this little girl entered her life and needed help as a foster adopt, it was like this incredible energy woke up inside of her.

With her curly brown hair and big blue eyes, Gisele was lucky to be alive. She was born prematurely with neonatal abstinence syndrome—a condition linked to her birth mother's use of heroin, cocaine, and methadone. The tiny baby was transferred to the hospital where Liz was working.

At eight months, Gisele had a feeding tube that went into her stomach for her nutrition. The nurse practitioner who was caring for her approached Liz and said that the baby needed to get outside. Being in a hospital her whole life wasn't healthy, and she was getting to a point where she wouldn't catch up developmentally.

"She was at this critical point. So I said, 'Well, I'll do it.' And at that point, the state was still working with her birth parents for reunification. But it didn't matter to me. I was like, 'This little girl needs me right now, and I need her, and we're gonna do this.' I just knew I could help her."

Three weeks later, Liz was filling her apartment with medical equipment to take care of the baby. She says she was all in from day one.

Liz took time off to get Gisele set up in her new home. "I was excited but nervous, realizing that I was committing everything I had to this child who might not be in my life for a very long time. I knew my love for her would never change, but there were times where I wasn't confident that we would be together forever."

Liz tells me that Gisele's birth parents were at first granted visits with their child. However, they weren't able to truly care for her, and their parental rights eventually ended.

Liz says she was thrilled that she could apply to adopt Gisele, but she understood the sadness of the situation for the birth mother and father. "They gave me the greatest gift of my life. And, you know, that was a struggle, because when I heard their rights were terminated, I thought it would be a sense of relief. I remember I was in my car at the grocery store when I got the phone call. And I started crying because I was so happy for two reasons. I had this beautiful, incredible little girl who was going to become my daughter. And then I imagined these two people, her parents, that just lost the same little girl. And it was a really tough day for me."

Bittersweet, I say.

On October 18, 2018, in a courtroom in Brockton, Massachusetts, Liz's dream of becoming a mom came true. Friends, coworkers, and family members were there to witness the happiest moment of her life. Gisele was hers. They were together as mother and daughter.

Liz was then given the documentation making motherhood official. There were photos taken, and Gisele grabbed the judge's gavel. Cheers, laughter, crying. A family celebration.

Liz tells me that Gisele's progress since then has been incredible. When she was first born, Gisele needed a ventilator and help with her lungs. She couldn't eat because she was in withdrawal from the powerful drugs her mother was on during pregnancy. Gisele developed an oral aversion to food, so nothing felt good when she was eating. She had gastric reflux and was losing weight, so the feeding tube was put in place. There were doctor visits, services, appointments with specialists. But the minute Liz took over, the baby started getting stronger. "She was advancing in everything. Socially, she was off the charts. From barely sitting up at eight months to walking at twelve months. Her lungs are strong."

The last thing Gisele needs to get rid of is the gastric tube that helps her eat. She's starting to love food, and over time, her mom is confident she'll have the tube removed.

Life is different from dreams, Liz knows now. Being a single mom with a demanding career requires stamina and balance. And love.

"I can't wait to see her wake up and say good morning. To pick her up at day care. To have her ask for her favorite foods that she could never eat . . ."

One of Gisele's favorite songs is "You Are My Sunshine." How perfect is that?

Before we end our conversation, I tell Liz how much her story has touched my life, and how I felt like I couldn't wait to talk to her and tell her story in this book. She tells me she believes we were meant to meet each other.

"I was supposed to be on *Fox & Friends* with Gisele to tell this story," Liz said.

"Oh no!" I say. "What happened?"

"I think something with President Trump happened, and we got bumped. We never got on."

"Oh *no*," I say again. "I'm so sorry!"

She says it was fine, but her dad, who is a huge *Fox & Friends* fan, was so excited they would be on. He watched it every day. So she had to break the news to him, and he was pretty bummed about it.

"Oh my gosh," I say. "I feel terrible. Can I send him something?"

Liz tells me he died in October last year, but that it is okay. She believes her dad had a hand in matching us up to put the story in this book.

I start tearing up as she's telling me about her father, and I talk to her about how being a parent has made me now more than ever want to live in the moment. You just never know what is going to happen, and that's why it's so important to appreciate the little things right now, in the present.

Yes, says Liz. That has been the biggest shift so far in her life.

"I think I lived my life for so many years looking forward and thinking what was going to happen next. I was stressed and worried. And now it's so much easier for me to live day-to-day. I appreciate being a mom and seeing her at age three and half. I just get so excited to talk to her, pick her up from preschool, and our bedtime routines."

There are birthdays and holidays, but Liz says it's the little moments that she remembers most. "Taking her to ballet class every Saturday morning—it's my favorite time of the week. Taking her shoes off and just tumbling on the floor."

Her family and her friends comment on how much more confident Liz is. "I have so much more energy because I can live day-to-day in the moment and appreciate what I have. Not to say that you don't think about the future, but that's not a priority anymore."

"It's the here and now," I say.

Liz admits that she would one day love to meet someone and have a relationship, but her standards are higher than they ever were because it's not just her. It's Gisele as well.

"Now I have the confidence to know what I deserve in a relationship. This little girl has given me so much. More than I could ever imagine. She has changed my life for the better in so many ways. I'm at peace. It's hard to describe."

I tell her I totally get where she's coming from. I say I thank God every day that I became a mom. Being a mother saved my life in so many ways. I never knew my potential.

My friend Liz agrees. She says she used to doubt herself in everything. Too old—too heavy—too career-focused. Her sister would point out that she needed to be kinder to herself and realize that being a mother was the role she was meant to fulfill.

"There was not one person that doubted that I could do it. But I did. And then when it happened, it was like suddenly, 'I can do it. I can do it, and I can do more.' And my career is getting better. All of it. And yet it's changed my life in so many ways."

Everything comes full circle when you finally realize your potential that everyone else saw before you did. When you're happy in your life, you notice the important things that you never did before. I tell her that, after children, I've been much more compassionate than I ever was. In some ways, I have more faith in God than I ever did. I ask Liz if she feels the same.

"Yes. You know what? I've always said I was raised Catholic, so I've always had that foundation. But I would say more spiritual, like I've always believed in God. I have always enjoyed going to church."

Liz's mom died when she was nineteen, and she was Liz's role model and why she decided to become a nurse. After she died, Liz found peace in the church and in helping her dad. She's always believed in a higher power, but being a mother has given it even greater meaning.

"You cannot deny to me this divine intervention. You can call it fate, or you can call it a higher power. But you can't deny how this has happened—this story of my life and how my baby girl was placed in my path."

I feel the same, Liz. It was meant to be. You and Gisele. A blessed family.

As we wrap up our phone call, I don't want to hang up. I tell Liz I want to meet her. This is one of my favorite stories, and I can't wait to write it and put it in this book of sunshine. You're amazing, Liz. What a lucky little girl Gisele is to have you as her mama.

"You sharing our story means so much," Liz says. "I'm so grateful for the opportunity to inspire so many people. I had no idea. I like that there's so many different aspects of the story that people can connect to. I never thought I'd have that opportunity in my life to touch so many lives. So, I appreciate you sharing us with others."

Liz and Gisele, thank you for showing us how important it is to take advantage of those opportunities when they present themselves.

———

DID YOU KNOW that being kind can actually make us feel better physically and emotionally? It's a simple rule: When you do something nice for someone else, it makes YOU feel better. It can be very simple. Share a smile, open a door, put a few quarters into a parking meter.

One of my favorite moments of kindness came from a person I didn't even know.

I have a favorite pair of sunglasses that I bought in Montauk last summer. They aren't fancy or very expensive, but I love them. They remind me of a happy place I visited with my family. I was riding the LIRR one day and misplaced them. I panicked when I didn't see them in my handbag. I knew right away that I'd left them on the seat of the train. I told my husband. Sean looked at me half-jokingly and said: "You'll never see those sunglasses again."

Noticing that I was clearly upset, he suggested I call the store in Montauk to find another pair. But I'd forgotten what brand they were and couldn't remember the name of the place where I'd bought them. I just kind of told myself to forget about them.

A week or so later, I noticed there was a lost and found at Penn Station (I never knew they had one, to be honest) and decided to go in, just in case someone had returned my sunglasses. The kind man behind the counter told me it sometimes takes two weeks for the items to find their way to the lost and found.

"But please come back," he said. "You have no idea the amount of stuff we get that no one claims because they think there's no way someone would ever take the time out to return their wallet, cell phone, or sunglasses."

And so I waited a week and went back.

This time there was a woman at the desk. I told her what I was looking for, and she asked me approximately when I'd lost them. She walked over to a blue plastic bin marked "sunglasses" (next to a bin of umbrellas, wallets, and other miscellaneous train treasures). As she was bringing the bin over to me, I immediately saw the sunglasses case right on top of a whole bunch of other lost sunglasses waiting to be claimed. My heart started beating quicker, and I found myself grinning from ear to ear. "That's them!" I exclaimed.

The woman smiled and told me I could have them back, I just had to fill out a document with my information. As I was filling out the form with my name and phone number, I asked if there was a way I could find out who had returned the sunglasses, so I could say thank you or give a reward. She said no, but she was sure that the person who'd found them would get paid back in return somehow. "Good karma finds its way back home," she said.

I'll never forget that stranger who returned my sunglasses. But, I realized, there was a chain of people who made that special moment happen. From the person who found them on the train seat to those who separated them from all the other lost items, the man who told me to check back in a week and not to forget, to the cheerful lady who finally showed me the bucket of lost sunglasses in which mine were at the very top. They all worked together to get them back to me. It was a group effort. I think about that all the time. Those lost sunglasses helped spread sunshine and, in the end, reflected it right back to me.

Chapter 9

CAN I TAKE YOUR ORDER?

Do you have a favorite restaurant, coffee place, or shop you really enjoy being in? Think about why that is. For some, it's the quality of the food or how efficient the staff are. But what about how *friendly* the people are in your favorite place? I've been to fancy restaurants, stores, hotels. But you know who gets my return business? The places where the staff are the friendliest, where they smile and make me feel happy. I've worked in the service industry. It can be tough to stay positive all day long. You're dealing with all sorts of people in different situations. It takes a special kind of person to put on a happy face and give all of his attention to customers.

That's why when someone goes out of her way to smile or be kind when dealing with clientele all day long, I tell her I appreciate her. In our third-floor cafeteria at Fox, my friends Curtis and Selwyn are the definition of customer service, going above and beyond their job description. They know everyone by name, and if they don't know your name, they ask, and they remember the next time you come with your order. You feel better after you see them and are greeted by their kind, smiling faces.

I've never seen either of them in a bad mood—and if they are going through something, you'd never know it. I see Selwyn first thing every morning, when I'm coming up to do my first weather report on the third floor. He's there before five a.m., setting things up. "Janice, good morning, my friend!" he calls out to me every morning with the biggest, widest smile. Throughout the day when I walk by, no matter how busy things are, Curtis and Selwyn will always stop and wave if they see me.

When I have friends or family visiting me at work, I always bring them to the third floor to have a bite to eat and to get first-class treatment from Selwyn and Curtis. They know my whole family and will shower my kids with attention. Theodore says Selwyn's fruit smoothie is the best he's ever tried. I told him the secret ingredients in that special drink are kindness and love. I don't say it enough, but it's people like Curtis and Selwyn who make the world a better place.

Malcolm Coleman reminds me why I love Curtis and Selwyn so much.

Malcolm has worked in the food industry for fifteen years. For the last five years, he's worked at Wendy's on the University of South Carolina's Columbia campus.

Malcolm hasn't had an easy life, but that has never gotten in the way of how he treats his customers, most of whom are students on campus.

In January 2019, a fire destroyed his home. He and his mom could no longer live there. They didn't have insurance, and the repairs were expensive. They didn't have a place to live and were staying in different places week to week. Malcolm also lost his dad not too long ago. Although he has many reasons to feel down on his luck, he never wants his troubles to get in the way of the people he loves to serve.

Robert Caldaroni, a student at the university, took notice of Malcom's sunny disposition. Once he found out that Malcolm was having a tough time, he decided he wanted to help. On a fund-raiser page Robert set up for Malcolm, it says: "Malcolm never complains and takes every day as a blessing. He clocks into work every night to continue taking care of his mother and puts a small portion of his check towards maybe one day being able to return home. Many people on campus know Malcolm because of his big personality and the unique ability to remember the name and order of every student after very few interactions with them. For years, Malcolm has gone above and beyond to care for students without expecting anything in return; now we have the opportunity to help out a friend in need."

I talked to both Malcom and Robert during the first few weeks of the pandemic. I ask how Malcom is doing. He says he's still working; cashiers and fast-food chains are still on the job, but the rules have changed. Malcolm says he takes this new situation very seriously.

"You just can't sit down. We've blocked off everything. You can come in, order your food, and leave. And mainly drive through. But it's been crazy. And now there's a curfew ban. You're supposed to be in the house at eleven, which is good because a lot of people are not really getting the grasp of what's going on. They're not paying attention, and people need that curfew to keep them inside. This is real."

I ask where Malcolm is living. He says he's with one of his aunts—his mom's sister. He's on the couch, and his mom is in another room on a cot.

Robert is also on our Skype call. He's back home in Middlebury. He's dressed in a tie and a jacket, sitting in his office (which is a closet he tells me with a laugh). I ask how he's dealing with school being closed in this pandemic we're all trying to get used to.

"I was abroad this semester in Valencia, Spain. And after a lot of the more hectic stuff happened, I was called back, and so I've been home. And my school's postponed, so I have a little break right now to get stuff done . . ."

I ask Robert how he came to know Malcolm.

"Just like most students at USC, I came to know Malcolm because I was needing some cheap fast food. [chuckle] And I've been going there because it's super-close, it's right on campus, right across from the business school, right on the corner."

Robert had been going to the Wendy's for several months, and the thing he remembered most was whenever he walked through the door, he'd hear his name. It was Malcolm. And he'd know Robert's order by heart. "It was the same thing for everyone—people would walk in, and you'd hear Malcolm call out their names, and you knew you were meeting somebody special. And over a couple of months, we'd chitchat every time I'd grab my 'Four for Four,' and we became friends."

I ask Malcolm what he thinks of the students. His face lights up. "Oh, I love them. I used to work at Russell House [at the university] back in 2014, before I came to Wendy's. I was a custodial worker, so I already knew many of the students already. I was unemployed for two years or so, and before that I was in the restaurant industry for a long time. But, Russell House was how I came to know a lot of these students. I love them all. They are beautiful to me. And for Robert to try and help me, I just cried when I found out. These beautiful people that wholeheartedly appreciate you as a person."

Malcolm adds that he's always been good at remembering names and faces. "I've learned that it hurts no one to take your time to extend yourself to people. And that's what people might be failing to realize. You just never know who might need to be seen or heard. And I can remember anybody's order, and I usually get that right, too!"

I ask Malcolm how Robert came to know the story about the fire. Malcolm tells me he was going through a lot. Not sleeping, trying to find places to live. Someone's couch or living room. Meanwhile, he was still working through all of the trauma over the last few months and trying to find solutions for him and his mom. It was starting to pile up. And then Robert came in one day and asked him, "How are you doing today?" Malcolm says he couldn't help it. It just came out: "Today, everything's piling up on me, Rob. I don't know how I'm going to do all this. My house caught fire . . . and on my birthday, of all days. I'm trying to keep myself together. Trying to help my mom. Do this, that, work here, feed the world. Save the world."

"Do it all," I say.

"It was crazy. And Robert. He listened to me."

The next day, Malcolm says, Robert came in and pulled him aside and said that the students wanted to help. They wanted to set up a fund-raiser for him and his mom. Would that be okay?

Malcolm couldn't believe what he was hearing. He gave Robert a free Frosty and said: "You gotta take this. Because I can't thank you enough." Malcolm adds: "And he has been a man of his word ever since he said what he's going to do. He has gone above and beyond, wholeheartedly put his soul out and networked. The whole crew."

I ask Robert what it was about Malcolm that made him want to help. He says what really impressed him the most is even though Malcolm was going through a painful time in his life, he never stopped smiling or being kind. Always making the students feel good. Even though you were ordering fast food, it felt like a home-cooked meal because your friend was handing it to you. He always kept his chin up, talked to you, smiled at you.

"Malcolm's work ethic and his friendliness, it's so rare. And he's such an awesome friend, and that's what you really feel like. He's a good friend."

From there, Robert called other students, and word spread. They made a video of Malcolm and set up a fund-raising website.

"I had a really great response. They see Malcolm. They see how great he is, and they want to help. So, it's not really been me. It's been Malcolm. When you're that good to a community for so long, there's goodwill that you can tap in to."

I ask Malcolm how his mom is doing. I say she must realize that she raised a special son.

"Well, she's a special human being herself. What you all see of me is a product of her. She and my sisters helped raise me. They led by example. They always treated people . . . well. I used to say to my mom, 'You know everybody.' I used to go in the store with my mom like, 'You know everybody.' I get it from her."

Malcolm pauses and adds: "You treat people how you want to be treated, and I firmly believe that. And I'm not perfect, I'm no saint. And I learned not to worry about what everybody else is thinking. I used to hate being so softhearted, and always wear my heart on my sleeve, but years ago I learned I gotta let that go and just be myself."

I say that's a good way to live. And a good reminder that we all need human connection to each other.

"We do. You never know what people are going through. I have very bad anxiety, especially all that was going on last year—heightened my anxiety and my depression. So, to hear that I do so much for them, but they don't realize what they do for me, spiritually, emotionally, and mentally."

Malcolm says it's hard for him to put into words what he means. "They do so much in return for me. They really do. For real."

Even though Robert and Malcolm haven't seen each other in the last few months, they still text and are in touch. I ask Robert what he wants people to know about Malcolm and why he decided to help him out.

"I just want the fund-raiser to serve as a reminder to all of the unsung heroes at our university. Because there's so many of them at University of South Carolina. The people that work there, the people that we share with. Malcolm's as much of a Gamecock as any of the students, and we really want everybody to know that. For nobody to feel disregarded. For nobody to feel like their work doesn't mean anything, because everything that everyone contributes really makes USC what it is, and every university, for that matter."

I tell them how much I love this story because after all that we're going through—the pandemic, the social distancing—it's a good reminder that we need human contact to survive.

Robert says he believes that, too. "People forget how good the world is and how many awesome things happen every day. How many great people leave the house, do a great job, leave a great impact on somebody else, and this helps remind everybody. For every dollar, Malcolm's probably put two smiles on somebody's face. So many awesome things happen every day, and I don't want anybody to forget that."

I see Malcolm getting emotional, hearing this. He adds: "I'm a proud black gay man in a society that sometimes has a hard time knowing what to do with me. I have fought to be him. To be me. They don't realize what I had to overcome, all the trauma I had to get through and still am working through. I had to fight to be this person. I had to fight to be me, and I realize, it's well worth it."

I mention that in so many of the interviews I've done with people doing extraordinary things for others, sometimes it's the ones who go through the greatest challenges that end up being the most grateful and the most appreciative.

Malcolm says, "Thank you so much. It means a lot to me that, like I said, they appreciate and love me and value me for me and embrace me. Someone said to me: 'We need more Malcolms everywhere.' I'm like, 'Really?' I had to think about that. And I'm still processing that . . ."

I tell him I truly believe that good things come to good people.

And he's right. We need to hear about more Malcolms in the world.

Chapter 10

VALENTINE'S DAY DELIVERIES

Seth Stewart loves Valentine's Day. But not for the reasons you might think. For the last nine years, the thirty-year-old has been spreading love on February 14 to strangers in his hometown of Spokane, Washington. His goal is to make sure that people who are missing someone in their life are not forgotten.

It started with just Seth and his brother. They heard girls complaining about being single on Valentine's Day and thought about doing something nice for them. Something simple, like bringing them a rose so they didn't feel as bad. They bought two dozen roses and gave them to people they knew. Word spread that they were doing this, and neighbors began asking, "Hey, can you deliver a rose to so-and-so's house or business?"

Messages started to pour in. Seth came up with the name "Rose Rush" and decided to create a Facebook page for others to "nominate" those who would benefit from the kind gesture. The next year there were a hundred deliveries, and it's gone higher every year. Now they're up to seven hundred rose recipients.

Seth likes to keep a list of all the women in his area to whom he delivers every year. In the weeks leading up to the holiday, he asks Facebook readers to send additional names of people who might need a pick-me-up so he can add them to the list.

I asked Seth how he pays for all of this every year. He says they've started a GoFundMe to cover the roses, and whatever isn't covered by donations, he pays for. This past year he printed shirts to make it more official.

When he gives out roses, he says, the recipients are usually very surprised. A few are standoffish, shy, or guarded, but every year there are people who are so grateful for the gesture, it's hard for them to put into words what it means.

Seth says, "There was one woman we delivered to this year. Her daughter explained that her mom had cancer, and she wasn't doing so well. She was wondering if we could bring her a rose. She followed up a week later, once we said yes, and it turned out this woman had just weeks to live and was taking a turn for the worse." They ended up giving her a bouquet of flowers, something they usually don't do, but for that particular customer, Seth says they had to go the extra mile.

"One elderly woman's husband passed away, and he had been gone a few years. Someone nominated her to have us bring her a rose and also requested that we write a note on it from her late husband. It said, 'Happy Valentine's Day. I love you. Love, Floyd.'"

Even Seth's girlfriend gets involved in the annual tradition. It takes a few days to sort through the messages and get back to everyone. Sometimes the emotion of it is hard to handle. "Not the workload," he says. "Reading the stories."

I ask about the girlfriend part of it: "Is she okay with you delivering flowers to strange women?"

Seth laughs and says past love interests haven't exactly been cool with it, and that's a deal-breaker for him. Some have definitely given him a hard time. He argues he can do his job and deliver flowers while also taking care of the person he's dating. "They see that I'm doing this for all these women across town: 'How can you make me feel special?' And I kept saying, 'I can do all of this and still make you dinner at the end of the night. Just be at my house at nine p.m.' I'm not kidding. I whipped up a complete steak dinner, mashed potatoes, everything, put rose petals everywhere. She walks in and sees I'm true to my word, surprised. And you know, in my head I say, 'I'm surprised I got it all done, too!'"

I mention to him that it's kind of awesome that he does this, and if I were his girlfriend, I'd be proud. He's making others so happy.

Seth mentions that all of the guys who drive around giving out roses say it's the best day of the year—delivering flowers even though they don't get paid. It means something to them. "It's impactful and it's incredible. It's not even just for the girls that get the roses. For the guys, they just like helping out, and giving back. But of course, the flip side to all this positivity was last year it went viral."

I ask why that would be a negative thing, being so popular and the word spreading about his wonderful business. He says just like everywhere else, there are trolls. They come out in full force, shouting on social media that he's doing this just to pick up girls. "They're all calling us 'Jodys.'"

I ask, "What's that?"

He explains it's the military slang for guys who hit on military wives and girlfriends.

Seth says that the last thing on their minds is picking up women. "Some of the girls that we deliver to are attractive, but some are really wounded. They've been through a lot. Many of them are seniors who have lost their husbands. Widows. Rough living situations."

Seth says the stories he hears are powerful and inspiring. "There are always people who break down and cry every year. Life has dealt them a sore hand or what have you. And some think they're destined to be lonely forever. Some keep the roses, and it's a tradition they look forward to. Some have even said that we've changed Valentine's Day for them forever. It's one gesture that lets them know they were thought of. Someone cares for them."

Some of the testimonials Seth sends me are beautiful:

My husband passed away several years ago from cancer. My granddaughter sent these boys my way a few years ago completely out of the blue with a rose on Valentine's Day. It really made my day knowing that someone out there took the time to make me feel special. They come back every year and keep a constant reminder alive that I'm not alone. Thank you, boys!

– Linda

My boyfriend was stationed in the Middle East, he personally knew Seth and what he does every Valentine's Day. He contacted Seth and arranged for one of his drivers to bring me roses from him, since he wasn't able to. Sweetest thing ever!

– Amber

I couldn't believe it at first. I'm a single mom of three trying to make ends meet. It's hard when it's just me. One of these boys showed up at my workplace with a rose and it meant so much to me, I broke down in tears! I was ready to give up on Valentine's Day and maybe even love itself. It really turned my day around.

And as weird as it sounds, my whole life! Gave me a new perspective to keep going and be happy. ☺

– Trisha

Seth tells me another story that his friend Eilish had a hand in: "We had just finished delivering on Valentine's Day this year, it was about seven p.m. Eilish contacted me and explained that her best friend, Nate, had passed away that week in a tragic accident. They were holding a memorial service for him the next day, and she was wondering if we had any extra roses we could give to his mother for the service. We had two bouquets of twenty-five roses left over from that day."

Seth says before he got the call, he was trying to brainstorm what to do with all the extra flowers. "We drove them thirty minutes away to her the next morning. They made a huge impact on the mother. I can't imagine a better way for those roses to be used one last time."

I ask Seth how long he's going to keep doing this. He says he hates turning requests down, but sometimes they have to, especially if it's out of town. His full-time job is running a landscaping company. But he does think about making Rose Rush a nonprofit so they can fundraise year-round. And there have been requests to start Rose Rush in other cities.

"I mean, shucks, I'm just a normal guy. Janice, you know, in my community, I do help out a lot, but I'm at my core just a normal guy."

I tell him that's why I think he's a perfect example for this book about making sunshine. He didn't start out to build an organization. He just took one thoughtful gesture and kept going, and it spread. One flower can make kindness blossom around you.

Seth then asks me what kind of book I'm writing and why I decided to do it. I explain that it's just a simple premise—to shine a light on positive stories like his that spread kindness. I tell him that when I was diagnosed with MS fifteen years ago, I could've used a book like this to help me through the dark times.

He says he's sorry about the MS and that he lives with diabetes. He's a type 1 diabetic, and it wears on him sometimes. I ask him if, because he lives with a chronic illness, that's why he tries to be good and kind to others or to find kind moments to make himself feel good. I tell him had I not been diagnosed with MS, I'm not sure I would've gone down this road of trying to find sunshine after some pretty dark moments.

Seth pauses and says: "Yes. And I will tell you something that I haven't shared with a lot of people. When I was diagnosed at eleven, I was bullied and picked on for my appearance, my lack of coordination skills, you name it. And it was really hurting me. I had just gotten diagnosed, and just got worse and worse, and I thought how could God love somebody like me when nobody else seems to care? And Janice, I tried suicide. I was a twelve-year-old kid. And I knew what I was doing, and I knew I wouldn't come back. But I didn't care. I just wanted the pain to stop. And so I loaded up three or four days' worth of insulin into me, and my parents weren't home. Nobody was home. I just injected myself. And my blood sugar was dropping lower and lower and lower. And I was starting to lose consciousness."

His parents came home just in time, and no one ever knew he was trying to kill himself. They just thought he was newly diagnosed, and it was a flare-up from being a new diabetic. Your pancreas sometimes goes into hyper-mode if you're not giving yourself any insulin. Sometimes it's an accident and you forget. It happens. But he says this time was not an accident.

"I didn't tell my parents until I was twenty-four years old. I fought with those demons and thoughts about killing myself for about a year. And then when I turned thirteen, I made a promise to myself. I don't care how hard life gets. I will never give up, ever."

Those thoughts disappeared, and they never came back. Seth says this time he is up for the challenge.

"I haven't thought about suicide, and since that day, I don't care what life throws at me. I don't care if I get slowed down to a crawl. I will not stop. And so that's what's fueled me to do good things. My mother raised me right. She's one of the kindest persons I know. She'd give the shirt off her back for anybody. And she's loved by everybody. My mom, my mom's just a saint. And so she instilled that into me to be good."

His dad is more of a tough-love guy and has taught Seth how to have a backbone. You need one these days to survive, he says. The combination of both his parents' traits helps him get through it all. He's always going to get right back up if he falls down. He says he's not the kind of guy to judge people by their cover. "I look at them and see why they are doing what they're doing rather than just pointing a finger and saying I'm better than them."

So that's part of the story, he says. He tries to look for goodness. Does what he can. Tries to do his part. I ask how he's feeling these days. He says he takes it one step at a time; he's been a diabetic for nineteen years now, and he's lucky. People rarely get this far without some kind of complication or hospitalization. He says his numbers could be a bit better as far as managing it, but day-to-day, he's fine. And he's grateful for that.

I tell Seth we're both lucky. He asks how I'm doing. I say, "Today is a great day. You never know what tomorrow may bring. Living in the moment. And right now I feel inspired, talking to you, Seth. Everybody's got something. You never know what a person is going through."

Seth says he's glad I found him. And he's happy we connected. "I knew in the first five minutes I'd like you," he says. I tell him I felt the same way.

Keep handing out roses and spreading that sunshine, Scott.

———

FOR NATALIE REILLY, Valentine's Day 2016 started off sadly. She was at home helping her mom, Hope, through her nineteenth round of chemotherapy.

"She was my rock. The strongest woman I knew, and she raised me to be just like her. But as soon as she got that cancer diagnosis, she turned into a shell of herself. I didn't recognize her."

Hope moved in with Natalie when she started treatments. She wasn't doing well, but not just because of the chemo. She was slipping into a depression and wasn't coming out of her room. Hope stopped eating, and Natalie says she was incredibly stubborn.

On February 14, Natalie was sitting on her couch feeling sorry for herself. Her kids were grown and out of the house. She was divorced and trying to help her mom. Nothing was going right for either of them.

All of a sudden, Natalie says she realized she was not being the person her mother had raised her to be. Natalie decided she wasn't going to sit and do this any longer. "I went in her room and I said: 'Get up, get dressed.' I knew she could. She had the strength, not quite the strength she had before, but she could still get out of bed."

Natalie told her mom they were going to do something that day. She had a drawer full of thank-you notes that were just sitting there. She threw them across the table and said, "It's Valentine's Day. We're gonna go leave notes on people's cars or give them out."

Her mom had a soft spot for veterans. And Natalie's son had been talking about becoming a police officer, so Natalie decided they were going to give valentines to veterans and first responders. They would both go out and look for them.

Her mom and Natalie sat for about an hour and wrote a bunch of notes. Then they got in the car and drove around. Hope didn't want to do it, and told Natalie so, but she endured.

"We drove around for three or four hours, and we looked for them. We went to the grocery store and found a Korean War veteran. He was in the frozen-foods section." Hope handed him the valentine and the hero started to cry. He was so happy. "He told us about his service, his late wife, and his buddies. He was just grateful for this one small thing."

Then Natalie and Hope drove around and left notes on police cars and trucks outside the grocery store. When they saw the license plate of a veteran, they got out and put a card on that windshield, too.

By the time they got back home, her mom was laughing and smiling. They were talking to each other again and discussing the future. They decided to do this every day. For as long as they had together.

"We'd get up, sit down, and write notes. I only half expected that it would do something for her. But it changed the last two years of her life."

Natalie saw that not only did it bring her mom back to her, but the returns she was getting from the community were also so rewarding. "I mean, I'll never be able to replace her. But I cannot imagine where I would be had I not started this, because the people that are in my life now, and the support and love they've given me, it's incredible."

I ask Natalie what she puts in her notes and why just the simple act of writing them is greater than we expect.

"To me, it's the magic in the handwriting and taking the time to sit down and do it."

She always writes to the veterans and tells them how grateful she feels for having her freedom, thanks to them. For their sacrifice and service. We don't know what they've endured, but we should be thankful. And she always adds that they are loved and appreciated.

The secret, she says, is to write to them like you know them so it doesn't seem superficial. "I picture my son because he's a veteran and a first responder now. And I always think, If I were writing to my son, what would I say?" That's where the power lies. It's not just a thank-you note. It's that we appreciate them.

That's what makes a difference.

Natalie says that it's not natural behavior to approach strangers and create conversations or give them anything unexpectedly. "I think, by nature, people think that you're gonna expect something from them in return. And when you don't, and you give them a note, there's always the look of 'What is this?'"

When you explain it, they're profoundly moved. Natalie admits she's had grown men break down in tears and cry in her arms. "You would think I had just discovered electricity, but it's something we can all do, and it's needed. It's not always easy to look at the bright side."

Natalie says she can't imagine her life had she not gotten up off the couch and stopped feeling sorry for herself, had she let her mom's life just go without further purpose. "I think that was it. She just needed to feel needed. To just get her out of bed. It changed things for both of us."

I ask Natalie if those two years with her mom were even more special now when she looks back.

"Yes. And then she really went out on her own terms. I think by the end of her life, she felt like she had done something with me. And on her deathbed, she made me promise to keep going."

The mother and daughter butted heads about different things over the years, but they remained very close. They were best friends. Natalie had gone through her own challenges as a divorced mom living with her two boys. She was focused on getting them raised and out the door. And suddenly, twenty years were gone. Dating was the last thing on Natalie's mind, but her mom decided to bring it up.

"I remember on her deathbed, we were talking about me dating again. And with her being gone, what would I do going forward. And she told me she was sorry, but she didn't think there would be a man out there who was going to get what I was doing—sending love notes to firefighters, police officers, et cetera. 'I'm not sure they are going to understand your intention,' she would say."

Natalie thought her mom was right, but she wasn't going to stop what she was doing. So she started praying. "There's a good man out there for me."

Her prayers were answered.

A year after Hope passed away, Natalie was invited to a high school football game. They were having a first-responders night.

"The football coach had me come in a few months earlier to speak to his football team—a hundred and fifty boys—about writing love notes! And so I brought in a couple of first responders with me, and veterans, so they could speak about the impact of the love notes."

This makes me smile. I tell her just the image of her talking to boys about writing notes is pretty funny and heartwarming at the same time.

"They loved it! Some of them cried. They all wrote notes to someone important that impacted their lives—a mom, a coach, a family member . . . And they did it. They really took it."

At the football game, Natalie met a retired cop. They were introduced, chatted a bit, and Natalie decided to write a note afterward saying it was nice to meet him. "He was down-to-earth and cares about first-responder health. I never thought about it again."

A few months later, they were reunited at a volunteer event, and they got to talking. He said he wanted to write a book about his experiences as a police officer, and Natalie told him she just happened to be a freelance editor.

The rest is history. They fell in love.

"The writing was on the wall," I joke.

Natalie says she laughs now because she remembers when her mom told her there wouldn't be another man. I tell her maybe her mom had other plans when she got to heaven.

"You know, I just feel like finding gratitude led me here."

I ask if she's going to keep doing this. How long does it go on?

Natalie says she can't let it go right now. It's like carrying her mom's voice.

"She was always the one who knew exactly what to say when times were rough, and those notes she gave were like that for a lot of people. A voice of reason and a voice of thanks. I know that I will never stop, because I know the impact it has on others and on myself."

Natalie still writes notes every day. It's cathartic for her. Sometimes it's not easy, and you have to make yourself do it, because there's nothing worse than going somewhere and seeing a police officer and not having a card to give to him or her. It haunts her.

Natalie says she's given out at least twenty thousand "Nothing but Love" notes.

I tell her I feel like we're losing this art form. The art of writing.

She agrees. And it's frightening. That's the reason she wants to pass it on. To go to schools and talk about being grateful and thanking others. Holding on to the tradition and the power of handwriting. "That's where the magic is for this mission."

I tell Natalie that I always keep a stack of note cards on my desk for any kind of occasion. Going shopping for cards is one of my favorite things to do. I was thinking about someone recently who had lost her mom several months ago. I took a card out of my stack, wrote how I had her in my thoughts, and sent it. Even if it's months following a tragedy, sometimes that's when you need to see an act of kindness. After the funerals and the wakes and getting back to some kind of normalcy, that's when someone might need words of of encouragement.

I also tell Natalie about the lunchbox jokes I put in my kids' lunches every day. I say it's hard sometimes to make myself sit down and find the jokes to write, but I do it because it's important. I want them to have a little piece of me at lunchtime, to know I'm thinking of them even though I'm not physically there.

Natalie tells me that when she was getting divorced and her oldest was in third grade, he struggled. He was seven and having a tough time, crying every day. He wouldn't let her go when she dropped him off at school; there was so much going on. She started writing notes on her son's napkins as a way of encouragement. A year went by, and she slowed down and stopped writing the notes because he was getting better and doing better.

And then . . .

"His junior year in high school, the last day of school, he comes home, and he brings his backpack home, and I'm going through it. And I'm going through his stuff, and in one of the pockets, there's a bunch of napkins stuffed in there. And I'm like, 'Billy, why are you saving all these napkins?'"

He told her he didn't have the heart to throw the notes away because they made him think of her. This made my heart sing when Natalie told me.

I mention there's just something about writing a few words on a piece of paper or a napkin that can mean so much. It's important to donate to causes and to give money to charity as much as we can. Those are tremendous gestures. And then there are the small ones that take a minute of your time and can be so personal and special.

Natalie says it's something that you can see, too. It's tangible. "Sometimes when you donate money, you don't really ever see what it's doing or where it's going. It's a one-way transaction. But this, you know where it's going, because you're handing it to them or you're physically putting it somewhere you know they will find it."

Natalie tells me a story that happened in a local Starbucks where she goes to write some of her love notes. "We're all in there, but nobody's looking at each other. They're all focused on their phones or devices. I see this young guy who's in his early thirties, and he's sitting at a table next to me. He was studying, and I was writing notes, and he had an army veteran cap on."

She quickly wrote him a note and got up and slid it across the table. She told him she appreciated his service and wanted to thank him.

He smiled and went back to studying. About an hour later, he got up and left. Ten minutes after that, Natalie says, he came back into the Starbucks to talk to her.

"He comes over to my table, and I look up, and his face is bright red. And he's in tears, his cheeks are wet. And he says: 'Ma'am, I had to come back. I read your note while I was in my car. And it took me a good ten minutes to get up the gumption to come back.'"

She says he could barely get the words out but wanted to tell her a story: "My name is Joe, and I served eight years in the army. I did two tours in Afghanistan. On the second tour, I lost my best friend. I watched him burn alive in front of me in an ambush. And I had to write home to this kid's mother to tell her about her son. But this note, your note, means the world to me."

In her mind, Natalie felt like she might've done something wrong. She hadn't wanted to upset this man. She thought, instead of being kind, it was bringing up terrible feelings of loss and sadness. Natalie told Joe she felt bad; she never meant for the note to bring all of those feelings back. He stopped her and said: "No, ma'am. This is what we need. Guys like me keep this stuff buried right here." He pointed to his chest. "We keep it all in here. Inside. And unless we let that go, we're worse off."

Natalie says the next thing she knew, she was crying. He was crying. "We're holding each other, two complete strangers in the middle of Starbucks. Nobody's really even aware of us. People are getting their coffees and leaving. You know, I never saw him again. But I won't ever forget his face. I will never forget his name and the name of his buddy who he lost that day in an ambush in Afghanistan."

We can't miss this stuff, I say. We have to acknowledge each other. Say hello. Smile at others. Don't get all caught up in our own heads.

"This saved me," Natalie says. "Having lost my mom, connecting with others saved me. There's not even a word for it."

I suggest "gratitude." "Thankfulness" and "empathy." All of it.

Then Natalie remembers something she did the other day. She now lives by a beach where cliffs look over the water. She took a stick and wrote in the sand: "You're beautiful." She walked up the cliff to see if you could see the words from above. A stranger was on the phone next to her and said: "I needed to see that message down there written in the sand. Today I was having a bad day. But that message helped."

A note in the sand that gets washed away eventually, but to those who see it, the message might stay in their memory for a lifetime.

When my fiftieth-birthday trip to Las Vegas was canceled, my husband figured out a way to bring "Vegas" to me.

Right: A FedEx driver from Boca Raton, Florida, took the time to disinfect a package to help a little girl that has an autoimmune disorder. Her mom, Carrie, wants to tell the world how it's the little things that mean so much!

Bottom left: FedEx driver Justin Bradshaw. (*Image courtesy of Justin Bradshaw*)

Bottom right: Garth Callaghan is a dad from Virginia who, despite battling cancer, has been inspiring his daughter, Emma, for over a decade with notes on napkins each day.

Above right: Janelle Boston has MS, and when she decided to share her biggest wish—to summit Mt. Tyson—it came true, thanks to the kindness of the Tully Rugby League!

Above left: Cheryl Hile didn't let her MS diagnosis stop her from chasing her dream of running marathons on seven continents.

Left: This kind mother, Beth Bornstein Dunningston, helped another mom and her kids at the airport.

Above: Passengers wrote advice on napkins that were made into a baby book for Mackenzie.

Left: Passengers created an impromptu baby shower on Southwest Airlines after discovering that a couple, Dustin and Caren Moore, were bringing their adopted daughter home.

Utah bride Kaley Young with her brothers, Kevin, Danny, Derek, and Kasey, and her husband, Andy Young.

Left: Kaley's dad, Dave, is in heaven and couldn't be at her wedding, but her brothers surprised their sister by adding a recording of their dad's voice to her wedding dance.

Bottom left: Robert Dunham, a fifth-grade teacher from Richmond, Virginia, turned the classroom into a barbershop to give his students haircuts ahead of graduation. *Bottom right:* Shannon Grimm, a kindergarten teacher from Willis, Texas, helped one of her students feel better about her haircut by getting a matching style.

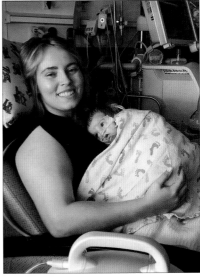

Above left and right: Florida Uber driver Belinda Smith cheered up passenger Nikki Ihus by taking her on a shopping spree for her sick child, John Henry. *Left:* Liz Smith is a nurse who adopted an abandoned baby girl, Gisele—a dream come true.

Bottom Left and Right: Students (including Robert Caldaroni, pictured bottom right) helped raise money for Wendy's employee Malcolm Coleman, who was down on his luck.

Seth Stewart and his buddies spend every Valentine's Day delivering flowers and making a difference one petal at a time.

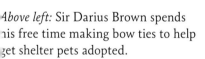

Above left: Sir Darius Brown spends his free time making bow ties to help get shelter pets adopted.

Above right: Natalie Reilly, from Arizona, writes "nothing but love notes" to first responders in honor of her mother, Hope.

Right: Compassionate kindergartener Katelynn "KiKi" Hardee and her mom, Karina, sell cocoa and cookies to raise money for others.

Left: Guy Bryant, a forever foster dad, takes care of over fifty young men, and they will always have a place to call home. *Right:* Romario, one of Guy Bryant's kids, feels lucky to have him in his life. *Bottom:* Alice Mayne gives senior dogs a new "leash" on life after a special pup changed her life forever.

Left: Gerard Dunn, a widower from Nova Scotia, Canada, got cards and wishes from around the world after his daughter made a request on Twitter.

Below: Tabari Wallace, a principal from North Carolina, made sure each of his seniors had a graduation to remember despite the pandemic.

ove: Heroic firefighter Ray Pfeifer made
re other sick first responders would be taken
re of even after his death. *Right:* Rebecca
ehra, an Olympic hopeful track star, helped
elderly couple too scared to go grocery
opping during the coronavirus outbreak.

Robertino Rodriguez is a healthcare worker who came up with a way that others can see him smiling even through his PPE, starting a movement in the process.

Above left: A famous athlete with a heart of gold, Tim Tebow believes helping others will always be his greatest priority.
Above right: Officer David Conley goes out of his way to meet every single student on campus and makes a difference in his community.

Bottom right: Mary Latham is a wedding photographer who spent three years on a road trip looking for kindness in all fifty states to honor her mom.

Chapter 11

GIVE EARLY, GIVE OFTEN

If you're a parent, what do you wish most for your kids? Of course, we want them to do well in school, have friends, be happy, and succeed in whatever they choose. But what about wishing for our children to grow up being kind?

I read a recent study where children were asked what *they* believed their parents were concerned about as they grew up. Their responses mostly said they thought their mom and dad wanted them to be achievers instead of being kind or good at caring for others.

In other words, they believed their parents were prouder of things like good grades or sports than if they were a kind person in their class or school.

Achievements are great, but being kind also has a big impact on growth and behavior heading into adulthood.

A good example of this is a video I saw a few months ago that had me in a puddle of tears. It was two friends playing baseball on opposing teams. One kid was pitching against his childhood friend who struck out, ending the game. The pitcher's teammates ran into the field to celebrate, while the pitcher decided to run over to his friend and hug him, instead. I saw an interview with the boy who struck out afterward, and he said although the loss of the game was disappointing, it was the kindness of his buddy coming over to embrace him that he would remember for the rest of his life.

That kind of empathy and kindness should be celebrated as well. What can we do as parents to foster that kind of reaction in our children?

Showing your kids that you practice what you preach is a start. You can also tell them, instead of "I want you to be happy" or "Do well on that test," "Don't forget to be kind to others." Studies show that those who express gratitude are more likely to be kind, helpful, compassionate, and forgiving later in life.

Dr. Robert Emmons is a professor of psychology at the University of California and is a leading scientific expert on gratitude. He writes: "I think gratitude allows us to participate more in life. We notice the positives more, and that magnifies the pleasures you get from life. Instead of adapting to goodness, we celebrate goodness. We spend so much time watching things—movies, computer screens, sports—but with gratitude we become greater participants in our lives as opposed to spectators."

Dr. Emmons uses an example of a woman in Vancouver whose family put their spare change in gratitude jars at the end of the day. By doing this, they gave themselves a regular reminder to focus on gratitude. When the jar was full, they gave the money to a good cause in the community.

Practices like this not only teach children the importance of gratitude but can show that gratitude compels people to "pay it forward"—to give to others in some measure like they themselves have received. Your hard work will come back to you in your children's behavior.

And if you'll allow me to brag about my own son for a moment . . .

A few years ago, my son Matthew came home from school and told me he wanted to participate in an event where he would shave his head to raise money and awareness for kids with cancer.

I was a bit surprised about the head shaving but not about him wanting to help others. I realize I'm biased, but my son Matthew is one of the kindest, most considerate human beings I know. He and his brother have something I believe you can't learn. They have the gift of empathy.

When we watch movies or read books that feature a main character struggling with being different, I can tell Matthew and Theodore take these particular stories to heart. They ask questions about why people are sometimes treated differently because of the way they look. I tell them you never know what someone might be going through, so it's good to be nice to everyone. They know that sometimes there are kids in real life who, at a young age, have big challenges to face, and that they're the bravest people you'll ever meet.

So while I wasn't surprised by Matthew's request, I did get a lump in my throat and had to hold back tears when I asked why he wanted to do it. He said that he felt so bad for little boys and girls who had cancer and lost their hair because of the medicine they had to take. It wasn't their fault that they looked different. He told me he learned about the St. Baldrick's Foundation in class, and despite being the only one who raised his hand to participate, he was adamant about doing it.

We all went as a family to the St. Baldrick's event that day. It was so heartwarming to see hundreds of young kids getting up onstage to have their heads shaved. One of the emcees of the event had a microphone and asked my boy why he was there. Matthew said, "I want to help others. I feel so bad for what they're going through."

Just seeing the number of kids with their shaved heads walking around in my neighborhood made me so proud. That act of kindness and charity spread through the whole community.

I HAVE READ countless other stories about kids doing amazingly kind things.

Five-year-old Katelynn Hardee is a kindergarten student at Breeze Hill Elementary School in Vista, California. According to Katelynn's mom, KiKi (as she's called) overheard a difficult conversation at school: another student's mother saying she was having a hard time paying for an after-school program.

Katelynn's mom, Karina Hardee, said her young girl started asking questions, wondering why things like this happen. "She's an inquisitive kid. I get hundreds and hundreds of questions on a daily basis. And she just started asking me questions about why the mom wasn't able to pay."

And then KiKi asked if there was something *she* could do to help. Karina told her that we have to be kind and give back to those who might be a little less fortunate than we are, even temporarily. Then Keke asked if they could do something to make money to help others.

"I had reminded her she had done lemonade stands over the summer. I was trying to teach her about money and saving. She could go get something with half of it and save half of it."

KiKi wanted to change it up. It was winter, close to Christmas. How about hot chocolate and cookies? Instead of keeping the money for themselves, she wanted to give it away to someone who needed it more.

The first week of December, KiKi and her mom sat out in front of their house and sold cocoa and cookies. After they were done, Karina says, "That moment about the after-school program turned into not wanting any of her friends to be hungry. That was her thought process.

She asked if she could donate to the kids for food so they wouldn't have 'grumbling tummies.'"

Karina and KiKi came up with a plan. KiKi helped bake the cookies and made the hot chocolate, then spent three hours over the weekend selling her homemade goods.

On Monday, her mom wrote a note to the school that said: "My daughter held a hot cocoa fund-raiser over the weekend and would love to donate the money to any of the negative accounts."

Katelynn's donation paid off lunch balances for 123 students.

I ask Karina where she thinks her daughter gets this compassion at such a young age. She tells me KiKi has always been that way: She asks questions about things that a young child shouldn't even be worried about. "I've had to find ways to already have harder conversations because she just keeps asking, and I don't want to lie to her. I just try to say it in a way that she can comprehend in her own five-year-old way."

Karina says wanting to give to the community has come back to her and gone to a place she never thought was possible. "There is a ripple effect here, and it's touched everybody in our community. We've received feedback from people around the nation saying, 'Thank you for helping. Thank you for being kind to others, bringing awareness.' And just having that platform gives her a little bit of a voice, trying to help where we can."

Karina says this has also created an awareness in her community for parents and their children. "It can be a small thing of an elderly lady that you help her take out the trash or you bring flowers to her. That kindness gets paid forward. Our community has come together with all of this pay-it-forward attitude."

I ask her how she does this all. Where is her superhero cape?

She laughs and says, "I have three full-time jobs now, but it's for the good of the community and the kiddos. She's kind of ignited something in me. I had it before I had kids." Karina remembers doing a lot of volunteering as a young person where she grew up in Northern California. To pass this on to her daughter has been such a blessing.

I hear KiKi in the background asking questions while her mom is talking to me. I ask her what she wants to be when she grows up.

She spells out: "M—O—M."

"A mom?" I say. "That's awesome."

And then Karina whispers to her: "What do you have on your papers when you're in Miss Ellis's class? What do you say?"

"I want to be a teacher," says KiKi.

I tell her how important a good teacher is in this world. They are one of the most important people we have. And moms are, too, by the way. I then ask her how awesome her mommy is.

She says: "Oh, she's a rock star."

I say that's about the highest you can go on the mom scale. I ask Karina how she came to know she had a serving heart.

"I was adopted when I was two and a half. And my journey when I was little impacted me. I have amazing parents who helped shape, encourage, and support me. And through the ups and downs, the community that I had, the people that supported me, was life-changing. I learned at a young age that even one person can touch somebody and help make an impact in their life. And so if I can do something with my own child, then I will try."

I tell Karina the biggest thing I've learned is it doesn't take a life change to spread kindness. All it takes is a momentary decision to be better. A smile, a wave, letting a person go in front of you who has fewer groceries than you do. Those things can spiral into something bigger—a chain reaction.

"Correct. And it does. It's only one small act of kindness that can make a huge change. I mean, from seventy-eight dollars at a hot chocolate stand and going into her elementary school to give them that after we held the fund-raiser. It's been amazing to watch what's kind of transpired and grown from it."

Watching other people doing something for someone else can be addictive. Athletes talk about a runner's high, but we don't talk enough about a "giver's high."

I ask where the future goes from here—what happens after cookies and cocoa.

Karina would love to run a nonprofit that helps pay off lunch balances one day. Maybe KiKi can help run it when she's older, if that's what she chooses to do. A lot goes into something like this, with funding and backing of other people.

"Time will tell. And if we can get a couple of, you know, big names or people in the food industry, somebody that can help support us, I would love for it to go beyond where it currently is someday."

I ask her if it's overwhelming. "Can all of this be exhausting?"

Karina says yes, sometimes. When people come and interview her daughter about her extracurricular activities, that can take a toll.

"She's been very candid about this. Like when others ask if she likes the attention. Her response is 'NO.'"

But then a follow-up question will be: "'Do you like what you're doing?' And her answer right away was yes. She's shy. She doesn't necessarily want, you know, all eyes on her."

The best acts of kindness sometimes are the ones that go unnoticed by other people. Just those who benefit from it know what's happening. That's powerful enough.

I tell Karina after we're done that the reason her daughter is so kind and compassionate is because of the great parenting she's done. She should be proud of that. Kind kids come from kind parents.

It's not always about what our children achieve but, more importantly, how they treat others along the way.

———

SIR DARIUS BROWN is someone who knows how to make his own sunshine. It comes in the form of a bow tie that he makes for pets so they can be adopted.

Darius is thirteen years old and believes wearing a bow tie can not only make you feel good about yourself, but it also might get the attention of others in a positive way. "Since I started to make bow ties, and when I wore them, I felt classy, dapper, more professional. It started to change my demeanor."

When I talked to Sir Darius for this book via Skype, he was wearing one of his beautiful creations.

Although he could easily make bow ties for himself or other people, Sir Darius decided instead to make them for adoptable pets so they would look cuter and more lovable to potential owners.

"When I was two years old, I was diagnosed with a speech delay, a comprehension delay, and a fine-motor-skills delay, which means I wasn't able to do things as easily, like tie your shoe or write with a pencil. I wasn't able to comprehend or speak well."

With the help of his mom, his sister, and some great teachers, Darius was able to overcome a lot of those speech comprehension and learning difficulties.

"Every day in school and out of school, I would always do my best to focus on how to accept and work on my challenges. I would come from school and practice speaking and writing. You know, small baby steps. I overcame those challenges. I feel like I don't even have them anymore."

It started by helping his older sister, Dazhai Shearz, who was interested in fashion. Darius cut fabric and learned how to use a sewing machine. Soon after that, he learned how to make bow ties. "Whatever my sister did, I wanted to do. So, back then, my sister was making hair bows for girls. When I'd come back from school, I would see her at the sewing machine. From that day, I wanted to help my sister, but I didn't know how. She allowed me to help her cut the fabric so that she could make the hair bows faster. Once I started to play around with the fabric, I realized I could make bow ties."

His love of making bow ties helped him overcome many of his learning disabilities. "It was a way to work on my fine-motor-skills delay. I had to use my hands in a weird way. It helped me adjust my hands."

When I talk to Sir Darius in April 2020, we're right in the middle of the early peak of the pandemic. I ask what he's been up to. He says he's been busy working at home doing schoolwork, reading books, helping his mom, and still making bow ties. He also decided to start making masks to help people on the front lines. At that point, he had made about twenty already, with a goal of a hundred to donate to a hospital or first responders.

I tell him I'm proud of him, and what a wonderful example he is for other young people his age. But what was that lightbulb moment for him? What was the motivation for helping others?

He tells me it began with something he and I have in common: weather and hurricanes.

"Hurricane Harvey and Hurricane Irma. During those storms, I noticed all the destruction that was happening, and I was very scared. But at the same time, I realized I wanted to help others. On the news, people were getting helped, but I didn't see any animals getting help. I was in tears when I saw the abandoned pets. We're all God's creatures. They also deserve to be in a place of love and cared for. What if I use my passion in making bow ties to help the dogs and cats find their forever loving homes?"

His mom, Joy, and sister, Dazhai, joined in to help turn his passion into something bigger. The first animal shelter where he donated bow ties was the ASPCA. "I have tons of adorable photos of me just having these adorable dogs in their loving home, living their best life, and I just couldn't be happier."

His love of making the bow ties gives those animals an extra way to stand out—just like Sir Darius. "I feel as though the dogs and cats feel cuter as they're wearing the bow ties, because they would love to play around with it. They just love to be so energetic and adorable when they wear my bow ties, and I just love it. And it's the cutest thing that you'll ever see in the world, really."

Sir Darius says he wants to help as many dogs and cats find their forever, loving homes and for them to live their best life. A little bow tie of kindness can make a big difference.

It takes him just ten to fifteen minutes to make a bow tie, and over the years, he's made hundreds of them.

I ask Sir Darius what he might tell another young person who wants to pursue a passion.

"Make sure you do it to give back to your community and not always focus on yourself. And do it out of the kindness of your heart, not because you're expecting anything in return. Because if you just do it out of the kindness of your heart, it makes you feel better as a person."

Sir Darius says he gets his compassion from his family. He says it's the women in his life. His mother is a "sweet and sensitive soul." And his sister helped him overcome challenges and encouraged his passion. "I really wouldn't be the Sir Darius that I am today [without them], so I'm very indebted [to] them."

I ask him what his plans are for the future.

"Making bow ties and helping rescue animals find their forever, loving homes." He also wants to expand into having pet foods and pet clothes, like shirts and pants.

I ask if he has any advice for someone who lives with challenges or stumbling blocks along the way.

"What I would say to a person similar to me is: Don't give up on yourself. Don't lose faith. Don't feel like you're different than anybody else, 'cause we're all God's creatures, He all created us equally. We're all amazing. We're all gifted. And . . . have that faith in you. Make sure you never give up."

I ask his thoughts about what we're going through right now in a pandemic. Is he optimistic?

"Definitely. I feel as though we're gonna be more prepared. For me, personally, I'm used to going to so many events and doing so many things. But now I'm home, staying home. We're all adjusting to it, but I am appreciating the little things that I have."

I ask him what he's grateful for.

"I'm grateful for my family. I'm grateful for everyone who gave me words of encouragement, positivity. And I just want to thank everyone who keeps on supporting me."

He's also motivated to inspire others around the world and looks forward to attending and speaking at conferences and events when things get back to normal. He wants to focus on the importance of education, volunteering, and giving back to the community.

He believes he can save the lives of animals, too.

"One bow tie at a time."

Chapter 12

FOREVER DAD

A lot of stories I've shared in this book are acts of kindness. I truly believe one small act of kindness can cause a chain reaction, and together those moments can impact lives in a big way. However, not every act is a one-time deal. Many people live that goodness day in and day out. How do they overcome the tests and obstacles that life brings? The answer is usually the allies they find along the way.

I remember this quote from someone I looked up to in my childhood, Fred Rogers: "We live in a world in which we need to share responsibility. It's easy to say, 'It's not my child, not my community, not my problem.' Then there are those who see the need and respond. I consider those people my heroes."

Guy Bryant, quite simply, is one of those heroes Mr. Rogers was talking about.

Even though Guy has no kids of his own, he's known to many as the "Forever Dad," having fostered over sixty children. Guy has been fostering kids in his Brooklyn home since 2007.

When I first talk to Guy (around the summer of 2019), he's feeling under the weather, like he's coming down with a cold. He's tired and achy, but he wants to do the interview and tells me he's doing everything he can to get better in time for the kids' vacation. He's taking four of his foster children to Atlantic City to have fun and go shopping together. They've been looking forward to this trip for a while, and he doesn't want to miss it.

Guy tells me he spent much of his career in children's services, but over a decade ago, he decided to become a foster parent.

"Back in 2008, I was working for the bed reduction program at ACS [Administration for Children's Services]. I met a young man who was really bright but didn't have anybody to motivate him. We had a good rapport, and he asked me if I could foster him. I had to give it some thought because I was living alone. And then . . . I just decided to do it."

I ask how that one situation developed into dozens more young men over the last few years. It turned out the first boy had a friend who needed a place to stay. "And then his friend had a brother. So he was coming around. That brother ended up moving in with us as well. And then they had another friend, and it just kept going and going. I finally had to move. And the most I've had is nine kids at one time."

Guy is a single foster dad. He divorced from his wife several years ago. I asked him how he handles it, being on his own with kids to care for.

"At first it was difficult because I felt closed in, like there was never a moment when something wasn't going on. But then I got used to it. I expected that every day there would be some kind of drama. And the day that there was no drama was a great day. So I just looked at it that way."

I ask Guy to give me a snapshot of one of the children he's cared for.

"There's one young man who many may have given up on. He came out of jail on a gun charge, and nobody would take him because people are scared—kids with guns. And when I looked over a file on him, they said that he was only three credits away from graduating from high school. And I thought this would be such a waste. And I took him. He did very well. He's management at a Starbucks now. He just bought a BMW. He has his own apartment. And I see him very regularly."

Guy says the boy's brother who was not in foster care, came to live there as well since he needed a helping hand. And now he's an IT tech at the UN. "He has his own apartment, and he has his own photography business," Guy says proudly.

Guy says all the boys he's taken care of have made an impact on him, even the ones who gave him problems. But he says he understands why these young men sometimes act out. "They just need somebody to understand and to pay attention to them." It's as simple as that.

I ask Guy what his upbringing was like. He says it was good. He remembers that everyone in the neighborhood would congregate at his family's home, growing up—"You know, on the steps [where] I lived in Brooklyn. It was a family house, and my aunts and uncles lived there, and we had lots of kids. I had cousins and a sibling, and it was always a big event. We went on bus rides. We did community stuff. We ran the lunch program from my home. We were always into helping people."

Guy says his desire to help others came from that close-knit family style he grew up with. They believed that everyone should have a chance.

"They don't turn their nose up at anybody's situation. And they used to tell me that you could be in the same situation someday. So, the help that you give now will prevent you from being in a situation later on, because you'll have an understanding of why people have these problems."

I ask Guy how he helps some of these kids he fosters. Is it as simple as putting a roof over their head? Being there for them as a role model in some capacity? He says it's not just he who makes an impact. Every one of us has it within to change and be a functioning member of society. He just gives them the means to get there.

"I will give you the tools, but you have to want it. I've had many successes. I've had a few failures. But you have to want it. And believe that you can do it."

He tells his kids that each day you live, you better yourself. And the day you stop bettering yourself, things are going to fall apart. "And I firmly believe that, you know, I'm there to catch you, but you have to better yourself so that you don't fall apart. I tell them that all the time."

I ask him what those tools are for success.

"Feed them, clothe them. Expose them to things they would normally be exposed to as far as vacation, trips together. And simple things like making them different kinds of foods. I get them to try things that they haven't tried."

I ask Guy if he knew this would be his journey someday. Were there hints along the way that he looks back on and realizes this is what he was put on the earth for?

"I wanted to be a dad. I was married, but we didn't have children. I was always good with kids and good with people who had difficulties. That's a knack for me."

Guy says he's able to relate to people whom others may not be able to see so clearly. Somewhere in that person is good, and it's up to other individuals to bring it out.

I ask Guy what it takes to be an ideal foster parent, and what advice he would give to someone thinking about fostering. Right away he says: Take the older kids first. "They are the most neglected of the population because people are afraid of what they hear and what they see. It's easier to take a younger kid and to try to develop them. But the older kids have been in many foster homes usually, and many living situations."

Guy says the older kids are loyal forever. If they know you love them and are invested in them, they will give that back. He remembers one time, when he was in the hospital, the child he raised who now works for the UN dropped everything and came to help. "He came to the hospital every night and stayed. He got me out of bed. He put me in the shower. He did all that. And when I came home, he came home from work every day and made sure I ate and everything. I'll never forget that."

He gave you what was given to him, I say.

"He definitely has. Over and over again."

I bring up a quote I heard Guy say in an interview that struck me. He said: "You could become a brain surgeon or you could be a bathroom cleaner. Doesn't matter. Once you come into my home, you're my kid for life."

"That's right," he says. "Yeah. I mean, more people, I wish, you know, had that."

Nothing means more to a child than being loved unconditionally. Family isn't blood. Sometimes we choose our own family. I have so many friends who I feel are my family more than those I share a name or DNA with.

"What people don't realize is that just like with your own kids, every kid is their own individual. It's even more pronounced with the kids that I service, because they've come from many backgrounds and they were raised by many different people and their values are all over the place. So, you have to get them to a point where they understand that this is the right way to do it. Get up. Get on your grind every day."

I ask Guy how long he's going to foster. He says he's sixty-two now, and he's been with the city for over four decades. He admits he's tired, but that doesn't mean he won't have kids in his life. He knows they'll always be around.

"My two oldest now are twenty-one, and the youngest one is sixteen.

So when the youngest wants to get out on their own, I probably will stop."

I tell Guy about an interview I did with Tim Tebow in which he said the most important work he does is going to see prisoners. He says he still sees value in them even when they've screwed up so badly that they're in jail. They are children of God. I tell Guy he reminds me of someone who sees the same in people regardless of where they come from.

"That is very important. It's the only thing that matters. Because if you don't feel they're important, you can't instill in them the importance of their life and the importance of them advancing. You have to see each kid for the values they have and for the potential that they have. And you have to be able to say, you know what? You can do this. I noticed that you do this well, let's focus on that."

I ask Guy to tell me about some of his proudest moments with his boys.

"My kid that works for the UN took me to DR [Dominican Republic] last year. My other kid that works at Starbucks took me on a shopping trip. Their graduations in school are proud moments, and when they get their own apartments. When they have their own place, I'm so proud of them."

Each of his kids still has a key to his home. They are welcome there for life.

Romario is one of Guy's foster kids and has been with him for three years now. When Romario was homeless, he was in a shelter, and Guy was the case planner assigned to him. Then Romario ended up joining Job Corps, a career program that helps young people get employed. He signed out of foster care but, five months later, was terminated from the program. He didn't have anywhere to go, so he asked Guy to take him in. His story, like that of many kids, is complicated. His mom was a single parent and having a hard time making ends meet. Romario got in trouble and told me he ended up going "somewhere for a while," but he was so glad Guy finally took him in. That was when his life started turning around.

I start off by asking Romario what it's like living with Guy. He says he's lucky. If you were a kid who went into the foster care system, this was the house you would want to live in. "He's very structured. He'll put you on a path of successfulness. All he wants with all his kids that he takes in is just to be successful in the future; that's all he wants, and that's really it. That's what it is."

I ask how long Romario can stay with Guy. He looks over his shoulder to ask Guy, who happens to be cooking lunch in the kitchen. Guy responds: "The foster care system will keep you till you're twenty-four."

Romario adds: "If you have a job."

Guy says with a chuckle, "Yes, I'll keep you till you're twenty-four if you're working."

Romario tells me when you first get into Guy's house, there are a lot of appointments you have to make. "Doctors' appointments, dentist appointments. He wants you on track at all points in time." Romario says he thinks of Guy like a father. They all call him Pop.

I ask Romario what Guy is making in the kitchen and if he's a good cook. Romario says yes. "He just made chocolate cake, and he made tacos and everything for everyone, all of us."

I say he's the real deal.

"Definitely."

I hear Guy laugh in the background.

I ask Romario if this experience he's in right now might inspire him to become a foster parent one day.

"That question is kind of hard for me to answer. Seeing the type of kids that you would have to deal with is kind of—it seems hard. It really seems like it's a hard job, so I don't know. I don't think I have the patience [chuckle] for it so much. But I mean, one or two kids, yes, sure. But like four, five, six, eight, no way."

I ask what he thinks are the qualities Guy has that make him a great foster dad.

"He's passionate about what he's doing. If he didn't want to do it, he would not do it, and he's sixty. Why would you want to be sixty years old and not want to live your own life? So I think that's passion right there. He's resilient, he wants to do this type of stuff. I don't . . . There's a lot of qualities, I just . . . I don't know how to say it."

Romario pauses and then says: "The house is family-oriented. We go on trips together, we have meetings with each other, we have dinners with each other, we even go see his own family. He brings us into his world, he doesn't have to do that. We sit down, we eat, we talk like a regular family would do."

I ask what the most important thing is that Guy can do for him. For his foster brothers.

"He's my support, so, my support system. If I had anything wrong or I'm questioning something, anything, I would just go to him and ask him. I would still be in a shelter if it wasn't for him."

I ask Romario if he has any advice for other foster kids trying to get on the right path.

"Whatever path they want to do, just make sure you get a support system. Make sure the foster parent cares for you. Talk to your case worker and change [him or her] if you have to, because you're not going to get nowhere if it doesn't start with the kid and the foster parent. It's a teamwork thing."

Romario has big dreams for when he gets older. He wants to be a fashion designer. It's what he's most passionate about. And he just graduated from high school.

"Congratulations to me!" he says, laughing. "I finally did it."

I can hear Guy cheering him on in the background.

As we end the call, I remember something Guy said in another interview I read before meeting him during our Skype session. The quote was: "Family is whoever is there for you. And whoever needs you. And whoever you need."

Guy Bryant, the Forever Dad, who will always be there for them.

Chapter 13

TEACHING OLDER
DOGS NEW TRICKS

You've heard the expression that we don't deserve dogs, right?

Just seeing our four-legged friends can make us smile and feel better. There's a reason why therapy dogs are so successful. They have the amazing ability to make us feel calm and reduce anxiety. Research shows that playing with or petting a dog can increase levels of oxytocin (sometimes referred to as the love or cuddle hormone because it is released when people snuggle or bond socially) while decreasing the production of cortisol (the stressful kind of hormone).

Alice Mayn loves dogs. All dogs. But the ones that take up the most room in her heart are the older ones.

Alice was a volunteer for Golden Retriever Rescue in California for many years, and from time to time she would take in foster dogs. She had a soft spot for the more "seasoned" canines. One day she got a call about a twelve-year-old golden retriever named Lily that was in poor health and was wandering the streets of Santa Rosa. Alice ran to Lily's rescue. That day, she says, changed her life.

Alice could tell this was no ordinary dog. Lily had a lot of problems. An infection in her nose, a tumor on her eye. But it didn't matter. Alice knew and felt in her heart this dog was an angel.

She took care of her, and Lily recovered. Still, as we've seen, moments of sunshine don't come without storms in between.

On Christmas night in 2007, Lily got a life-threatening illness called canine bloat. Alice rushed her over to the emergency center, and the doctor took her in. They told her they needed to operate right away. Miraculously, Lily bounced back. She was a joy to have around. Everyone who met Lily felt her energy.

Unfortunately, her health issues continued with a seizure. At the end of February, Lily came down with a blood disorder. Her weakening body was taking on too much. Alice believes Lily knew it was her time to go. She died peacefully on her bed with plenty of love around her. Despite being with Alice for only four months, Lily would impact the rest of her life.

Alice recalls the day after Lily died. It was that day she saw a different path for herself. An epiphany. "I was doing something in the house, and all of a sudden I thought: Lily's legacy." Alice foresaw a dog sanctuary to help other dogs like Lily. "A place where senior dogs who are lost, abandoned, or homeless will have a safe haven where they will receive love and care that they deserve."

It's because, Alice says, Lily gave that love back in ways that surpassed her own dog years on earth. "When Lily passed away, the message I got from her was that 'There are a lot more dogs out there like me, and they need help, too.'"

Alice founded Lily's Legacy Senior Dog Sanctuary in Petaluma, California. Lily's Legacy provides a home for senior large-breed dogs until they are adopted or until they pass on.

Finding a location for a dog sanctuary wasn't easy, but Alice believes Lily had a hand in helping find a place for other dogs like her. "It's not easy when you're telling the landlord of a place you want to rent that you want to run a sanctuary for dogs. There's usually a click at the end of the phone when you tell 'em that."

Alice finally found the perfect property as soon as it came on the market. It was five acres, and they closed in thirty-two days. "You don't close on a property in a month in California, but it was meant to be. That was Lily helping out."

Alice tells me about the time they needed a van to transport the dogs with volunteers to the vet. She sends out a letter twice a year, and one of the supporters called and said they had a van.

The list got even longer for things they needed. "We wanted a pool—swimming is a great exercise for senior dogs—something above-ground that we can put a deck around so the dogs can get in and out."

Alice says she talks to Lily "up there on that Rainbow Bridge" when she's thinking of other things they may need. She says those thoughts often turn into sunshine during times of darkness.

After she prayed for a pool, she opened up her email again, and there was one ready to be donated.

I tell Alice that when you do good things for others, it comes back to you.

The shelter's goal is to be able to rescue at least 150 dogs per year and house twenty to twenty-five at a time.

"Over the years, I've developed a relationship with many of the local shelters. So the volunteers call me when they have an adoptable dog they know won't be leaving."

Alice says that larger dogs are surrendered to shelters due to health problems the owners can't afford to pay for. Other dogs outlive their owners and have no place to go except the local animal shelter.

Each resident dog gets to live in a room with its own direct outside access in a fenced area specifically for that dog. Also: "We have a big exercise field behind the yard in the back."

While all the dogs are welcome to live out the rest of their lives at the sanctuary, Alice says, what they really hope for is forever homes.

Claire is a dedicated foster mom. On the Lily's Legacy website, she talks about why it's important to foster:

> When I tell people that I foster dogs, they always say, "I could never do that. It would be too hard to let them go." And it's true. It is hard to let these sweet seniors move on. Whenever that time comes, I remind myself of the positives.
>
> They finally find a home. They won't have to bounce around, and they will be loved. Mostly, though, I think about my next temporary pup. I don't know where they've been or what they've experienced, but I know I can give them a comfy bed, lots of love and belly rubs until they find their home, things they might have had to go without in the past. For me, it's much more heartbreaking to think of another dog in need than it is to let one you love go to a new, loving home.

I ask Alice what it is about these dogs that she loves so much.

"Well, there's a lot of history. There's a lot of research about having dogs and how it helps everyone. A house without a dog to me is just empty, no matter how many people were in it."

And, she adds, the dogs are so grateful. "Gratitude is the thing I have learned about these animals. I've always been a grateful person, but no matter what they've been through, and I've seen some horrific situations, these dogs are grateful and come to you."

Alice tells me about a dog they took in that was so badly neglected, and she was the sweetest thing in the world. She was left outside in the backyard and forgotten. Left alone. So sick, but when you showed her love, that she was wanted, she would give you a kiss every time she saw you. Her tail wagging was her way of saying thank you over and over again for loving her.

"When I see what's happened with Lily's Legacy and where we are today versus where we were when I started in my backyard ten years ago, it's just mind-boggling. The first we took in after Lily was named Miracle. We've been having miracles ever since."

The benefits of owning an older dog are numerous. Alice wants people to consider the older ones if they can. Adopting may first and foremost save their life. By taking in a senior dog, you are not only providing it with a better life, you're also saving it from being put down. Of course, everyone wants a puppy, but many don't realize how much work the young dogs can be. It's like having a baby. Senior dogs are typically already trained and know basic commands. They are potty-trained. Adopting them will save you time and energy toward training your dog.

Contrary to the popular phrase, you *can* teach an old dog new tricks. They can be trained at any age, and older dogs are just as smart as the young ones. Seniors have a greater attention span than a puppy, which makes them easier to teach.

Older dogs are calmer and less energetic—less destructive to your home. Many of them do well with younger kids. And they make wonderful instant companions.

"The older people that adopt from us love the older dogs because they're companions as opposed to a hiking buddy. I mean, not that some of our dogs don't do hiking and adventures, but there is a multitude of stages that fit into a person's life when they get to be fifty-plus."

Alice adds that of families who have young children or teenagers and adopt from her, almost everyone has mentioned what a good experience it's been for their kids to learn about caring, respecting, and understanding the elderly. You see what their needs are and what they still have to offer.

She says they couldn't run Lily's Legacy without their volunteers. "No one gets a dime for the work they do. They're a very devoted, dog-oriented team of volunteers that are just selfless people. I mean, there's no politics around here. It's all about the dogs. We have two or three of them at once on site, all day, every day, seven days a week, from ten in the morning until six at night. And two of us live on property. Those dogs are never alone."

They also have people who come into the shelter called cuddlers, a group of people who just come to snuggle with the dogs while reading a book or sitting on the couch. This makes me smile.

Alice says they do extensive research into the families who want to foster or adopt. They have a seven-page application, two home visits, and reference checks with their vets and with their friends and associates. "We have a very, very low return rate. I don't think in ten years we've had more than five or six dogs come back to us."

Alice says this work has made her realize how grateful she is in her life. "I've certainly had my challenges in life, but now I've got four wonderful children, and they're all adults now. The dogs bring it back to you in spades."

Alice adds that although the sanctuary is geared toward senior dogs, the lessons that people can learn are things they can carry on in life: "If you could be kind to a dog, then you can be kind to your neighbor. You know, kindness begets kindness. It's a wonderful way to live."

It's amazing how many obstacles dogs can brush away with a simple wag of their tails.

Chapter 14

HAPPY BIRTHDAY, GERARD!

A few years ago I was scrolling through Twitter and came upon a post from a woman named Miriam living in Cape Breton, Nova Scotia. There was nothing fancy about it, no pictures or videos attached, but it caught my eye. It had been retweeted several hundred times. It read:

ATTENTION FRIENDS: Since Mom died this past Spring, my 92 YO dad waits for mail every day. Listens for the squeak of the mail slot opening. His BDAY is Oct. Please mail a note, card, picture, map or story!

The address was included on her tweet, and it captured my heart in an instant. I tweeted back to Miriam: A card is on its way!

She wrote back: Thanks, Janice!

I had a pretty card in my desk drawer with a rainbow on the front that was perfect. I wrote:

Dear Gerard,

Happy Birthday! I hope you have a wonderful day, month and year. We love Nova Scotia. My mum Stella was born in Newfoundland! Your daughter Miriam told all of her friends on Twitter it was your birthday, so we all wanted to send our best wishes. If you're ever in New York, I'd love to meet you in person.

With Love,
Janice Dean xoxoxo

My card would be one of close to five thousand that landed at the home of Gerard Dunn in the weeks and months after Miriam's request for birthday messages.

Miriam says when she sent the message, she figured she might get a dozen retweets. But her post inspired thousands. After she went to bed that night, she woke up to over twenty thousand retweets and announced: "Dad, you're about to get a lot of mail."

Boy, was she right.

She called the post office and told them they were about to get very busy. "They said: 'It's okay, dear. That's what we do.'" Miriam announced this might be a different kind of situation.

The first day there was one piece of mail.

The second day there were three.

The third day there were twelve. The carrier announced: "Wow. Twelve pieces of mail. That's awesome."

The fourth day the postman told them there was a truck on the way.

I kept in touch with Miriam, smiling at all the articles and videos sprinkling the Internet from news outlets all over the world and the "Birthday Card Request for the Senior Widower" story.

I asked Miriam if I could write about her dad in this book of sunshine, and she gave me her blessing. It's hard to deny the love her parents had for each other. Her father showed it every day.

"He would say: 'Doesn't your mother look beautiful?' She could be wearing her housecoat with her hair uncombed. It didn't matter."

He also left hand-written notes:

"I love you."

"Be right back."

Miriam says seeing that kind of affection from her parents made her expect it from a partner.

Whenever Gerard walked through a room, he went out of his way to touch Ellen's shoulder as he passed by. Just a little tap. A gesture of kindness and endearment. "Hi, Mum," he would say.

Ellen and Gerard were together over sixty years.

"He played the piano, and everyone sang along. Except Mum. She would just listen and then say: 'Oh, that was lovely, Gerard.'"

She always complimented him on his playing. He played every day. Miriam would ask her mom what the secret was to a happy marriage. "She would say kindness." Miriam asked her dad the same question. "He would say consideration. You have kindness and consideration that never forgot itself. That was part of their lives every day. It was a beautiful relationship to watch. They did so much for each other."

Miriam's mom died unexpectedly on a flight home from Sarasota, Florida, where she and Gerard were snowbirds for thirty years. Ellen ended up having pneumonia even though she didn't feel sick. On the plane, Gerard thought she was asleep and kept fixing the pillow around her neck. She had been up all night packing, so he thought she was just very tired and needed to sleep. Then he realized he couldn't wake her up. The head flight attendant looked for a doctor on the flight, and because there was no ambulance on the ground yet, the crew decided to keep the plane in the air until one came. They circled the airport a few times and delayed landing. When they touched down, Ellen went immediately to an ambulance and was brought to a local hospital. She was put on life support, and she died eleven days later.

The reason Miriam tells this story is because if it hadn't been for her dad's birthday wish, the stewardess on that flight would be plagued with guilt for the rest of her life.

"I received a message from the flight attendant after the press had caught on to Dad's birthday extravaganza, and she wanted to reach out to tell our father first off that she could see the love between the two of them on board." Miriam pauses. "You know, before the incident happened, they were sitting across the aisle from each other. The tenderness and care that he gave her. She remembered it."

The flight attendant couldn't stop thinking about the pilots' decision to keep circling around the airport before landing, and she kept wondering if it was the right one. Because of that, and the guilt she felt after that day, she went back to school and enrolled for more medical emergency training. The letter she wrote to Miriam's family was heartbreaking. But Miriam knew exactly what her mom would've said. She told her she did the right thing.

"Mom would be very proud of her, that she went back and got more education, because that was the most important thing to her. Mom was a teacher, a doctor of education. This gave the flight attendant—it gave her peace."

Guilt is a big emotion when it comes to overcoming tragedy. We spend so much time trying to replay or change up the story in our mind about how things "might" have gone had we done something different. You can't close off those thoughts, but you can redirect them. You can lean in to them and use them to put your energy into something else, like the flight attendant did.

When Miriam told me this story, I spent a long time thinking what a gift this was for the flight attendant who might've spent the rest of her life torturing herself for a decision that she can never go back and change. But from that point onward, she chose to better herself and learn from what had happened in the past.

I asked Miriam how she came up with the idea of getting strangers to send birthday wishes to Gerard—on Twitter of all places. She says she and her siblings had worried about his loneliness since their mom had passed. Ellen was his entire world. They had seven children together and many grandkids. They were inseparable.

The siblings wondered what they could do to fill their dad's day, and one answer was: MAIL.

Every day he would listen for the "squeak of the mail slot." It was the highlight of his day. It occurred to Miriam that since she followed some lovely people online, maybe they'd send him a piece of mail to keep his spirits up. His birthday was coming up, so she thought she would request some cards via her Twitter account. What happened next was incredible.

"I expected six to ten cards. And then it was shared and retweeted dozens and dozens of times."

Miriam stayed up all night. She was excited but nervous, too, thinking her dad might not like that she'd asked complete strangers to send things. What if her siblings thought it was irresponsible to post his address?

Thankfully, her worries were unwarranted. The whole family considered it one of the most extraordinary things to ever happen. They believe their mom had a hand in it from heaven.

Gerard was particularly moved by the hundreds of messages from schoolchildren from around the world. They were all so sweet, positive, and heartfelt. Then there were the hundreds of personal stories and pieces of art. The many photographs of babies, grandkids, and pets. It seemed so intimate. There were moving letters sent from cadets in officer training who poured their hearts out. Gerry (as friends called him) had briefly served in World War II.

"There were more gifts than he received in his entire lifetime put together. Some were small, trinkets, fridge magnets, key chains. But some were large and came from extraordinary places. A handmade shirt from Ghana; a quilting guild for the Calgary Police Department made him a quilt."

One message Miriam says she will never forget. She noticed one card in particular that said: "Happy Birthday, Dad."

It was from a woman who had purchased a card for her own dad's ninety-second birthday, but he passed away before she could give it to him. In her note to Gerard, she said she'd kept the card, for some reason, and when she read about him and the request for birthday messages, she knew she had to send it.

"He got choked up. Dad was so moved. He was like, 'Imagine that.' It wasn't the number of cards or where they came from in the end. It was the stories, where it touched people, where they felt a piece of themselves."

Those are the things that he loved the most and what Miriam is grateful for. The sentiment was much bigger than just sending a card to someone.

Another note read: "Thank you, Gerard. Thank you. You saved my life from drowning when I was a little girl."

That woman had waited and waited and thought she'd never get the chance to tell him that. And then she had the chance. He remembered her, and was glad she was alive.

Miriam says, "Another woman told me that she had never sent a card to her parents in her entire life. She was in her sixties. And after sending one to Gerard, she decided she was now going to do the same for her parents. It changed her life."

Because of Miriam's request for her dad, writing letters and cards is now happening in schools. Children send them to seniors' homes.

There have been so many happy consequences from this story that keeps giving.

Miriam says the little birthday project was something pure and simple: people wanting to make a connection.

These thoughtful notes kept Gerard company and gave him great joy until, almost a year before his ninety-third birthday, he, like his wife, passed away of pneumonia.

"And we know he loved life so much that he wasn't ready to let it go," says Miriam. He would get sick and then get better. Doctors were astonished that he kept recovering.

This went on for a couple of weeks. Finally, Miriam says he asked for his family's permission. He said: "I think it's time. I want to go see Mom."

"We replied: 'Okay, Dad. That's what you want. You know, then, we don't mind. That's what you should do.' We were all with him for the last two days. We sang songs and were holding his hand. Singing one of his favorite songs, Linda Ronstadt's 'Blue Bayou,' when he passed away. He used to play it on the piano, and I would sing it."

Miriam said he had a beautiful life. And a lovely death. Filled with love and music.

Miriam took to Twitter to tell the world that her dad had decided to peacefully move on, not struggle anymore, not use any heroic measures, and just "go see Mom."

I told Miriam that when I saw the news of Gerard's passing, I felt like a member of my family had passed away. I reached out to her and told her how sorry I was and how deeply it had affected me.

She told me that so many felt the same way.

Miriam received more cards and letters after people heard of her father's death—many celebrating his life and thanking her for sharing her dear dad with the world.

"It was not something that happened and was forgotten," she says. "It continued to be part of our lives, and it really meant a lot to him. It made him very happy, and it made him feel not that he was special but that the other people were special. People changed because of my dad's story."

Looking back on this, Miriam says her tweet caused a "ripple effect," with many people telling her that they were inspired to write letters to their own elderly family members or to reach out to others who may be in need.

The greater meaning for her, she says, is how open people are to love one another. Much more so than we typically think.

"Somehow the message developed that the world is a cruel place, that nobody wants connection, that people are antisocial. But it is not true. The world is filled with love and goodness waiting for a place to show up. We need to allow ourselves to be more vulnerable, and therefore more authentic, and risk sharing our love with others. That's the best of humanity."

As for how Gerard felt about the experience, he was both humbled and proud, and he never lost sight of how thoroughly special every single card, letter, or gift was. He felt loved.

"Six months before my mom passed, my husband died. And, as you know, just eleven months after the 'birthday extravaganza,' our dear dad left us. That is a lot of loss. But when I think of my loved ones, I don't always feel pain. I feel something else. I feel happiness. Because that love never leaves us."

And it takes only a few moments to sit down, write a note, and tell someone that you care.

Chapter 15

PRINCIPAL WALLACE

Many of us who have young children have been homeschooling since the pandemic began. And even though I had such a huge respect and love for our teachers before coronavirus took over our lives, I am even more grateful for their dedication to their profession after having lived through this period of time.

My husband and I have seen so many emails from our teachers to parents and kids telling us how much they miss the children, miss seeing their faces in the classrooms. First and foremost, this epidemic has taken a toll on our elderly and those who care for them. But few others have had it harder than children and the people who love them. No playdates, no recess, no field trips, no birthday parties. Their parents took on many roles, such as friend, nurse, teacher, and babysitter in addition to their normal duties.

Even the older kids missed out on the end-of-school concerts, field trips, plays, proms, and graduations. Many of these events were canceled and were not rescheduled. Some parents came up with ways to celebrate despite the restrictions. Kids posted videos of their recitals, plays, and concerts done at home. Some parents got their graduates to put on caps and gowns and have their own living room ceremonies.

North Carolina principal Tabari Wallace is someone who wanted to make sure his seniors got the recognition they deserved, and the promise of a graduation at some point, so he organized a personal celebratory parade for the graduates at his school.

The West Craven High School principal decided to dress up in full cap and gown and visit his seniors one by one with a stack of yard signs personalized with each student's face and the message: "You will graduate." As Principal Wallace placed each sign in a yard, he asked students: "Please accept this as a token from the Craven County Board of Education, administration, and teachers until we can finally get you across the stage."

Principal Wallace was someone who needed to be highlighted in this book.

I start our conversation by asking Tabari what he makes of the testing of all our skills, patience, and limitations during this pandemic. What did he tell his students and teachers?

"I'm trying to lead by example and let them know this, too, shall pass. It is extremely frustrating for the students—and the teachers, for that matter. I think they're getting more frustrated than the kids are. But we just try to keep everything calm, letting them know we're going to work through this. 'We got you, just keep doing work, and we'll take care of you at the end. That's all we can ask you to do.'"

Tabari Wallace has been a principal for sixteen years. He says he's been nicknamed the "Journeyman of Craven County." They keep moving him to schools that need to be turned around, that are having difficulty. This is his third school, serving as principal, and he's made a success out of every place where he's been. I tell him he must have the magic touch. He says he got lucky in most cases but that he prides himself on investing in human capital. Fortune 500 businesses are results-oriented, always trying to put their resources where they will have the most impact. The results will take care of themselves.

Principal Wallace says he didn't choose his profession. Education chose him. His first master's degree was in rehabilitation. He was playing post-collegiate football, and his former football coach at his alma mater called and said, "You wanna coach?"

He agreed, started coaching, and then became a math teacher. He did that for four years and was hooked. "Those kids experiencing in the moment of that joy when they overcome a challenge, or they learn something new that they didn't know, and they jump in your arms and they hold you, that's it. That's the bug. That is infectious. It will bite you and you cannot leave. And here I am, twenty years later."

I ask if he had a favorite teacher growing up whom he remembers having the bug.

"I did, I did. Her name was Ms. Green. She was my chemistry teacher, and she was tough, and she said something to me that still sticks with me today. She believed that I can do anything and that I was the first football player to ever make an A in her chemistry class."

I ask how that motivated him. He says it just made him go forward.

"My parents always instilled in me: 'If you want to get out of where we are, education is the key, and you're going to have to work hard. Nobody in this world is going to give you anything, so you need to work for it and earn it yourself.' That's why I'm so big in this equity thing, opportunity for all. You have to do it. You have to want it so you don't have to come back here where we are, and you have to want to get out of where I grew up, then keep pushing forward."

Tabari grew up in Five Points, New Bern, in North Carolina. He was living in the Craven Terrace Projects, and then his family moved over to Duffy Field, which was on the other side but still Five Points. He says it's still very working-class. He was there until he left and went to Greenville for college.

I ask if his parents were always telling him to do well in school. Is that where this attitude comes from?

"Yes, and I'm kind of jealous, because the world has changed. Students and kids today have so many rights. We had no rights coming up. If the school called, you're in trouble. Mom didn't even wait to hear what you did in school! If that school called, one time I got it, and it was something good they were calling for. But we were just conditioned that education is so important. In order for you to change your circumstance, you have to go out, and you have to complete it."

He tells his students that the key is to do well in school. You don't want to answer to your mom, like he did, if you don't do your work. That's what his mother instilled in him. She showed him you have to meet deadlines, always do your best, always be an asset. Never become a liability. Make the most of every opportunity that comes in front of you.

Tabari is from a family of three boys. All three of them graduated from college.

"Mom only graduated from community college with an associate's. So she's so proud, and I'm proud of what my brothers have become. My younger brother owns his own business here, he owns every taxi in New Bern. God has blessed my family. We're not supposed to be where we are today. But we're successful, and I thank God for that. I feel it's still a privilege to sit here and talk to you and to be given the platform that I have, because I'm just so lucky. I just don't know how it happened, but He took care of me."

I tell him that yes, it was hard work, but also drive and doing well in school. Not to mention being a good person.

"You said it. And I tell my kids this because the character piece is even more important than the intellectual piece. That's what really opens these doors for you so people can see your true intellect."

Tabari lives by the saying that people may forgive what you say and forget what you do, but they will never forget how you made them feel. You always remember those life moments when someone might've made you feel bad, or maybe they made you feel amazing!

"Through leadership, I always make sure I tailor my message, to make sure I'm being positive and passionate and that they know I truly care for their well-being and for their platform."

I ask him where the graduation idea came from, to go to everyone's house. He tells me the district made the signs and left the delivery up to the principal. One school let the resource officer plop them in the yard and walk off. The other two asked some teachers to put them in the yard and leave. His school was the only one that put together a parade for the students, bringing the graduation to their houses. He says, "I thought to myself, Well, shoot! They can't come to us? They didn't say we can't go to them!"

He wanted to help fill that void created by the pandemic. "The class of 2020 has been through so much, and that's the least we can do, is to let them know that we care, we're here with them, and that eventually we will get them across the stage."

Fourteen groups, led by a caravan of teachers, coaches, police officers, firefighters, and community leaders, visited 220 seniors from West Craven High, covering 485 square miles, taking a total of four hours.

What would he say to all the kids out there going through this challenging moment?

"It's an old saying that when you plant the seeds of a tree, it's thirty years before you would get to enjoy the shade that it produces. And I would advise to all the students, not just the class of 2020 but everybody, that even though you're in a different environment, you're not at the school, you're not without your friends, this is short-term. And that we will get through this."

Because that's such good advice, and a pep talk for students, I ask him to give some guidance to parents going through this with their children. "Please, Principal Wallace, give me your expertise!" I plead with a smile.

He laughs. "Poor things. I tell y'all to just be patient. Just to know that we're here for you to help you get your child over the hump. We ask you to be encouraging to your child and really to take care of yourself, because it's tough going from Mom to a teacher. But in order so you can keep your sanity, make sure that you do things that you like to do when you're not helping your child with the instruction. And never hesitate to reach out to the school. We're only one call away."

I tell him he's absolutely right, and at our school, both the teachers and the principals have told us the same thing. We're not alone, and they're here for us. That has been constant.

Principal Wallace reminds us that out of all tragedy comes some form of triumph.

I ask Tabari about his family. He's married. He and his wife have been together since the age of sixteen. They were high school sweethearts. She's a principal of an elementary school in Havelock, North Carolina. They are both in the final-dissertation phase of getting their doctorates. He tells me their daughter graduated with an advanced degree.

"She's [Tabari's wife] a property manager in Greenville. We weren't supposed to make it—according to experts, we would never make it because we started out so young—but God, I gotta give it to Him, He has blessed us so much that, again, we're where we are today."

I want to know more about the importance of investing in our kids. And how critical attitude is. Principal Wallace says it's all about the relationships we foster.

"If me and you had to put a table together and the boss came in and said, 'All right, Janice, you and Tabari put this table together, and I want it done by five o'clock today,' all right, we'll put a table together, but most likely, it's not gonna stand. It'll fall in two weeks. But if we put that table together with love, you were invested in it, you had a seat at the table in the design of it, you knew where we were going with it, and you were appreciated for what you do, then that table would never fall."

Tabari says that's the true secret. You have to invest in your relationships, and the students have to know that you care and you're going to have their back.

"The teachers have to know that when they need you, you're there. I have an open-door policy. And it's an ongoing love-based projection, is what I call it; love-based theory is what I follow."

I ask him to tell me again what he said to each graduate when he visited them all at home and presented each with a personalized sign to put on the lawn.

"We told them to let this sign serve as a bridge. Every time you come in and outside of your house, you look at this as a reminder that the community, the staff, and the Craven County Board of Education is going to get you across that stage to graduate no matter what. That's our mission."

That reminds me of one of my favorite Emerson quotes about educators: "The great teacher is not the man who supplies the most facts, but the one in whose presence we become different people."

Or, to put it a little more succinctly, "If you can read this, thank a teacher."

Chapter 16

RAY OF LIGHT

Everyone knew our friend Ray Pfeifer was dying of cancer. But his diagnosis came from saving others, and his legacy will live on, helping those dying of the same. I call his cancer the hero kind.

Ray Pfeifer was a presence. I don't remember the exact day I met him, but I felt, as many do, that I always knew Ray. Sean brought me by the firehouse when we first started dating, and Ray was the one guy you couldn't resist. Quick to joke, easy to talk to. So kind. People gravitated to him. He owned the room when he walked in, and incredibly, he could disappear when no one expected it. He called it the Irish goodbye. The guys called it "the Ray." You could be having a conversation with Ray, beer in hand, turn to look away for a moment, and he was gone.

My favorite memory of Ray was when I had just moved to Manhattan and I was living on the Upper West Side. I was walking home on a sunny warm NYC day, crossing West Sixty-sixth Street, when I noticed a commotion.

A crowd of people had gathered near the crosswalk. I scanned the area to see what was happening. I saw a fire truck and some yellow tape cordoning off the area, then noticed a familiar face. Actor Tony Danza was at the corner of West Sixty-sixth and Broadway, coming out of taping of his talk show at the time. Wow, Tony Danza, I thought. I was new to New York, so this was considered a celebrity sighting. But people weren't looking at Tony—dozens of onlookers were gravitating toward the fire truck. I looked past Tony Danza and then heard a chant of one name:

"RAY!"

"Hey, RAY!"

Lo and behold, it was my friend Ray Pfeifer. I later found out Ray had dropped off his chief at a meeting, and while waiting for his boss to finish, he was going to drive up to his old firehouse where he worked with my (then boyfriend) Sean. There was a call on the dispatcher's radio that they were at an incident near Lincoln Center, so Ray decided to go and take a look.

As the crowds circled around Ray, I realized that Ray Pfeifer was my New York celebrity sighting (no offense, Mr. Danza). I slipped by Tony and joined in, waving and calling out Ray's name. He came over with a wide smile and gave me a hug. This was before he found out about the cancer that was spreading inside of him.

Ray spent twenty-nine years as a member of the Fire Department of the City of New York. He always said he was excited from "day one" up until the last day he worked. Every single minute. He was proud every day to put on the uniform. He announced it was a "great way of living."

HIS SLOW DEATH began on September 11, 2001, the day our country was attacked. Nineteen terrorists hijacked four airplanes and slammed two of the planes into the North and South Towers of the World Trade

Center. A third plane went into the Pentagon in Arlington, Virginia. The fourth plane crashed in a field in Shanksville, Pennsylvania.

Thousands of people died that day in lower Manhattan; 343 of them were FDNY firefighters. If you have never lived in New York, you can't imagine what that's like. When just one of New York's bravest dies in a fire, it's front-page news for several days.

Ray and my husband, Sean, worked together at Engine 40/Ladder 35. They lost twelve of their men that day, every working member. For many of them, their remains were never found. Americans referred to the wreckage as Ground Zero, but for everyone in lower Manhattan, it was the Pile.

Hundreds, if not thousands, of firefighters and other emergency workers worked day and night on the Pile, sifting through debris and glass, breathing in toxic fumes, trying to find their lost brothers. Ray did it for eight months.

Ray's cancer was diagnosed in 2011. It was later attributed to his time on the Pile. More and more men and women who were down at the World Trade Center site came forward with similar symptoms. Doctors were finding out this wasn't just "normal" cancer.

After the Twin Towers fell, a layer of dust and debris covered Manhattan. Hidden among that cloudy air, inhaled by survivors and first responders alike, were carcinogenic particles and chemicals—asbestos, fiberglass, mercury, and benzene, among others.

Starting in his kidneys, the cancer spread everywhere in Ray. It eventually took his leg, and in April 2017, in his last few weeks, Ray was transferred to hospice care, suffering from brain cancer, with cancer in his nodules, lungs, and adrenal glands. Ray says he was one of the lucky ones. His friends, he said, were murdered on 9/11, but in the years he was alive after that, he got to watch his kids grow up. For that, he was grateful.

When Ray found out about his incurable illness, his mission became not only to beat it but to raise funds and awareness in Congress that people like him—those who did not die on 9/11 but who would eventually die from the effects—needed to be cared for. The evidence was piling up just like the toxic waste these guys sifted through after the dust settled on that fateful day.

More than eighty thousand responders with cancers linked to the 9/11 attacks were enrolled in the Centers for Disease Control and Prevention's World Trade Center Health Program. Ray banged on doors with his cane. He called members of Congress. He steamrolled his wheelchair to Capitol Hill to stop leaders in the hallways and tell them they needed to help. There would be no Irish goodbye. He would be kicking and screaming until they did something to extend the James Zadroga 9/11 Health and Compensation Act (named after a New York City police officer who died of respiratory disease attributed to his participation in the rescue and recovery at Ground Zero). It was a law enacted that guaranteed medical care for 9/11 first responders. Ray earned a key to New York City for his dedication to getting that job done. And after his death, the Zadroga Bill was made permanent. An FDNY EMT who knew Ray very well said outside of his wake service that the act "may be called Zadroga, but it was Ray's fight."

Several years later, Ray's name was added to the Zadroga Bill to give balance not just to what it took to get it passed but what it took to get it extended. His name, along with that of NYPD detective Luis Alvarez, who also testified on Capitol Hill before his death, is now part of it: "Never Forget the Heroes: James Zadroga, Ray Pfeifer, and Luis Alvarez Permanent Authorization of the September 11th Victim Compensation Fund Act."

"I was just a poster boy," Pfeifer said when he was honored at New York City Hall with the key to the city in January 2016. "We got something done . . . It was hard-fought. We dealt with people that didn't really get it."

While in hospice, he still managed to raise seventy thousand dollars to buy a transport van for other sick first responders. He was saving others while he was dying.

The FDNY has a total of thirty-two family vans. They're all funded by private donations and used to transport firefighters, EMTs, and their families to doctor/hospital visits. Each van is named after a fallen hero. Ray and his family used them to get to his doctor visits. Ray decided he wanted other firefighters who needed transportation to use his van when he didn't need it. He couldn't stand it being idle when others could also benefit from its use.

Ray said he didn't want to die and then have his family ask for the van in lieu of flowers. He wanted to do it before he left this earth. "Nobody gets out alive in life. If I can pay it forward by getting a van and wherever else I can help out to be a voice, it's important to me."

"And now I'm going to live forever," Ray said, talking about the van with his name on it.

One of his last wishes was to lay a wreath at the Tomb of the Unknown Soldier at Arlington National Cemetery. It was to honor those who have fought and died for America, before and after terrorists struck the Twin Towers.

He felt a kinship with some who gave all.

Ray liked to message me often during *Fox & Friends,* a show he loved to watch. "Watching you now, kid. You're doing great!" he would say.

When Sean told me that Ray was getting sicker, I sent him a picture of my family at my son Matthew's first communion that simply said, "We love you Ray." He texted back a thumbs-up. It was the last I heard from him.

A few days later, my husband gave me the news. "Ray's gone," he said quietly. The lump in my throat is still there as I type this. We all knew it was going to happen, but that didn't make the news easier.

The world needs sunshine, but the earth needs rain. Not everything turns out the way we want it to.

Ecclesiastes 3 (made even more popular as a verse in the Byrds' song "Turn! Turn! Turn!"): "To every thing there is a season, and a time to every purpose under the heaven: A time to be born, and a time to die. A time to plant, and a time to pluck up that which is planted."

Ray's funeral was like him, larger than life. Hundreds gathered at the Holy Family Church in Hicksville to bid a final farewell to a man who mourners said was the true definition of living a life of kindness. He worked until the end to help fellow first responders.

Sean and I were there, along with Ray's family, firefighters, and friends. Ray had been friends with comedian Jon Stewart since they'd met lobbying for health benefits for sick first responders. Mr. Stewart fought back tears when he talked about the collection of prayer cards Ray always carried with him from the countless funerals he attended. He used them as inspiration while he fought for their care.

"The irony here is Ray would've loved a day like today, where people from all over—town, city, the country—pay respect to a man who did right," Stewart said. "Make no mistake, Ray Pfeifer died in the line of duty because of illness in the terrible terrorist attacks of 9/11, but more importantly, Ray Pfeifer lived in the line of duty, now and forever.

"Now, Ray, I've got yours"—he held up Ray's prayer card—"And it's going to teach me how to do right."

Like Jon Stewart, I carry Ray's prayer card in my wallet. I tell Sean it makes me feel safe, like Ray is watching over me. My guardian angel, my "Ray of light."

His sister Maryellen says Ray was always a "doer." He had a way of "sucking you in." Once you were in, that was that. "You were locked into a world of doing good for others, too."

Ray's legacy will last longer than any of ours will. He will be remembered for fighting cancer and fighting to keep others alive.

His mantra was: "Do the right thing even when no one is looking."

Those words are written on his foundation website and on the Ray Pfeifer family van.

My husband, Sean, spoke on behalf of Engine 40 and Ladder 35 at Ray Pfeifer's plaque dedication a year after his death. Sean stood in his uniform and talked about Ray, the man he was, and his twenty-seven years of service with the fire department.

"On the morning of September 11th, 2001, Ray heard about the attacks and immediately raced back to New York with other members of the house in a few short hours, linking up with other off-duty members of 40/35. We dug for our fallen brethren until dawn the next day, and then on successive days that turned into weeks and finally months on hallowed ground that slowly transformed from the Pile to the Pit.

"Ray, as our de facto sergeant major, pushed us to attend services, dig downtown, and care for the families of lost members. Ray let others be one of eleven family liaisons, and he became more of the firehouse liaison and adviser. Though we did not admit it then, we were also trying to renew our souls, and part of that renewal was knowing when truth was more important than fact—some may call it faith.

"After 9/11, Ray was quick to say that the FDNY was *still* the greatest job in the world, which seemed delusional then, but he knew that was exactly what we needed. He ensured that tragedy did not also break our spirit, and it turned out to be true.

"Ray saved his best for last. He was not the first firefighter to head down to Washington to push for the Zadroga Act extension, but he was the most formidable. Ray loaned his voice, his spirit, his cane, and later, his wheelchair, to a seemingly impossible cause—when all else fails, call Ray.

"There was only one Ray. He was same person in the firehouse kitchen, at the union hall, at a fire, on the Pile, at headquarters, at the fort, receiving the Key to the City, talking to a general, or in the hallways and offices of our elected officials. The only thing that ever changed was Ray's widening influence."

Everyone deserves a Ray in their life. We're so lucky we had him in ours. Gone but never forgotten, the "Ray of light" that comes from heaven always lets us know he's watching over us and reminding us every day to do the right thing. Even when no one is looking.

Chapter 17

GROCERY DELIVERY IN THE BEGINNING OF A PANDEMIC

I know I quoted Mr. Rogers earlier in this book, but honestly, if ever a person knew exactly what to say to help us put our minds at ease, Mr. Rogers was the GOAT.

One of his most famous sayings was about the helpers: "When I was a boy and I would see scary things in the news, my mother would say to me, 'Look for the helpers. You will always find people who are helping.' To this day, especially in times of 'disaster,' I remember my mother's words and I am always comforted by realizing that there are still so many helpers—so many caring people in this world."

His wisdom applies in many situations. Parents sometimes don't know what to say to their kids when asked about tragedies or sad news going on in the world. I've used it to talk to my kids, and since my husband is a firefighter, I tell them their dad is one of those helpers.

Rebecca Mehra from Oregon is also a helper that Mr. Rogers told us about.

Rebecca's tweet in early March was one of the first I remember seeing that made a big impact during the first few weeks of the pandemic.

The first case of confirmed COVID-19 in the U.S. was found in Washington State. In January of 2020, a man had reportedly returned from Wuhan, China. He had a four-day history of cough and fever. The patient said he had seen a health alert from the CDC (Centers for Disease Control and Prevention) about the novel coronavirus outbreak in China, and since he had some symptoms and had recently come from that region, decided to get checked out.

At the end of February, the virus began to spread more rapidly in communities all across the U.S.

The first death came on February 29, when a woman in her fifties died with a preexisting health condition. The second person was a man in his seventies, who also had health issues and was living in a long-term nursing facility near Seattle.

Rebecca was walking into a Safeway in Bend, Oregon, to pick up a few things after track practice when she heard a lady calling to her from a parked car. She went over and found the woman and her husband, in their eighties, asking for her help. She shared the experience on Twitter afterward. She wrote:

> I walked over and found an elderly woman and her husband. She cracked her window open a bit more, and explained to me nearly in tears that they are afraid to go in the store.
>
> Through the crack in the window she handed me a $100 bill and a grocery list, and asked if I would be willing to buy her groceries.
>
> I bought the groceries and placed them in her trunk, and gave her back the change. She told me she had been sitting in the car for nearly 45 min before I had arrived, waiting to ask the right person for help.

She added:

I know it's a time of hysteria and nerves, but offer to help anyone you can. Not everyone has people to turn to.

Her tweet was shared hundreds of thousands of times.

A chain reaction began across the country of others wanting to help, too. They just needed to see someone leading by example.

I talked to Rebecca a few weeks after her tweet was first shared, and she told me this moment was the first time she had thought about how the virus was affecting her neighborhood. Back in early March, Bend had just had its first case of coronavirus. Rebecca had heard it was making older people sick. The grocery stores were already seeing shortages of toilet paper and hand soap. Rebecca says there were aisles of cleaning items that were empty, but she was able to get most of the groceries from the elderly couple's list.

When she got home, she called her boyfriend to tell him what happened. He encouraged her to share it with others on social media; it might help someone. Millions of people saw it, and the comments were also in the thousands.

When I talked to Rebecca, she had just found out the Olympics were postponed. She's a runner, and she was planning to take part in the Olympic trials for track and field in June. The games were supposed to start July 24.

I tell her I'm so sorry to hear this. She says she was disappointed but that she understood. "There's a public health crisis. And I'm lucky I'm a distance runner, so I can still run outside, but so many athletes are affected and can't do their normal training. I guess I'm lucky."

I ask how she's handling this. She tells me it's been challenging in different ways. Her boyfriend and she have been together for five and a half years. The last two years, they haven't lived in the same place.

She's been training in Oregon, and he works in the San Francisco Bay Area. He was planning to move to live with her, but because of the pandemic, they were probably going to hold off on that chapter of their lives for a little while longer.

I tell her it's moment-to-moment reality right now, because if you think any further from today, it will make you go crazy. Rebecca agrees, saying that now more than ever, it's about living in the present and appreciating the little things.

"Because it is really is nuts right now, especially as an athlete. We've been waiting for news on the Olympics, what's happening with the Olympic trials, what are we training for, when do we get to race next. And that's our livelihood. What comes next is truly not known."

Rebecca and I talk about how, even though we are in such a scary moment in history, moments of kindness are really bringing us a tremendous connection to one another. Her tweet was a window into what we were all about to experience. She says it was just a routine visit to the grocery store after practice. She walked in to get basic dinner items. As she was walking through the parking lot, she heard the woman yelling from her car, and Rebecca skeptically walked over to where the voice was coming from.

I ask if they exchanged information.

"I felt bad afterwards that I hadn't given her my name. I could have written my phone number down in case she needed anything else. The good news is there's now this whole infrastructure set up in my town to help people like that, who don't feel like they have a choice or don't feel safe to go outside. But at the time, this was all just really starting and hitting central Oregon, so yeah . . . a regret there."

I ask how she decided to write about it on social media.

"I wasn't going to say anything about it. I told my boyfriend about what had happened, and he said, 'Oh, you have to post about it.' I'm not much of a Twitter user. I got a Twitter account six months ago, so

I said, 'Okay, fine.' And I tweeted it, and I never could have expected the kind of response that I ended up getting. It was crazy."

I tell her, for me, her tweet was one of the first huge wake-up calls. Others felt the same way. There were thirty-five million views. Rebecca was shocked, but looking back, she says, the most impactful thing was not only people reaching out and saying thank you but people reaching out and saying, "Hey, I don't know if you know anyone in this area, but I'm willing to help people get groceries in Kansas City, Missouri." Then she would get other messages from Kansas City, Missouri, saying, "I need help." Rebecca says this was a call to action for her.

I ask if she found the couple who handed her their grocery list.

"No. I would have assumed that they would read the local newspaper or have seen something on our local news, but I also know that it's a really crazy time for people, so I'm hoping that I get connected with them eventually."

I ask Rebecca why she thinks the woman picked her to trust with money and a grocery list. Does she think there's something about her, a way or a manner that makes her stand out among others? I tell her I find that there are many moments when we find strangers along the way, placed in our path for a reason we'll never know. At the time she didn't think anything of it. She admits she was thinking of all the hard work she had put into her training that might now get canceled, and that she could lose her job. Selfishly, she realizes, but the moment she talked to the elderly couple who were afraid to go into the store was the moment she became aware that she was the lucky one.

Rebecca says she didn't even think twice. She was just happy to get the groceries for them. Many people have asked her if she was afraid they had the virus, but even if they did, Rebecca says, in a time like this one, you need to do all you can to help those around you. She didn't hesitate.

I ask Rebecca whether she felt a little "feel good" reaction after she got the groceries for the couple. I told her I had read that doing acts of kindness can set off a similar reaction to what runners refer to as a runners' high.

"Kind of an adrenaline feeling, you mean?"

"Sort of," I say. "This kind of good feeling, like you did something important. How did you feel afterward?"

"When she'd asked me, I was initially so shocked and surprised that this had happened. The coronavirus was starting to become a reality for our community. And I didn't really think much about it while I was in the grocery store. It wasn't until afterwards, after I gave them back their stuff, and I felt this sense of relief because I saw the relief on her face, that I really reflected on it."

She tells me that this was a good thing but also something we all need to be doing for each other. Especially for those being hit the hardest.

Rebecca's tweet became even more important than just awareness. She was helping others connect in other cities, states, towns and countries.

"I tweeted about this on a Wednesday evening. And I noticed it was starting to get traction. I had six hundred Twitter followers, so that was very surprising. And by the time I woke up the next morning, I had thousands of messages on Instagram, Facebook, and my Twitter. As the story grew and had national attention, there were folks from different countries asking: 'Could you help me? I'm from Naples, a town where most people are over sixty-five years old. We're really getting hit really hard. But I own this grocery cart, and I need to get people their groceries. How do I do that?'"

Rebecca had the help of others—a sponsor from a women's athletic brand, friends, her boyfriend to assist with managing her account, requests, messages, and questions. They've all been doing the best they can to connect with everyone they can. She says there's been a large impact in her community in Bend. A Facebook group called Pandemic Partners was made with thousands of people getting involved and posts every day, from "Hey, my family is in quarantine, we're out of milk, can you help us?" to people who are in the hospital, who need pickups, and everything in between.

Rebecca says she loves that all of this has evolved from her one act of kindness and others taking action to pay it forward.

I ask if this might set up a different path for her in the future. She's an athlete, but maybe this is a higher calling in a way. Rebecca says she's been interested in public service for much of her career. She also works for the mayor of Bend and was an international relations major in college, spending summers in public service internships. Many of her family have also worked and still work in public service.

"Even when I'm not connecting people to help each other, I've been doing a lot of helping the mayor, trying to get the information out to people in Bend, and make sure people feel safe and understand what's going on. That's definitely something I've always valued."

I tell Rebecca that her story is really the basis of why I'm writing this book. Sometimes organizations and movements can start with a plan to go big and affect millions of people. However, sometimes it's just one person doing one small thing. Her one tweet caused a massive call to action. I saw hundreds of stories after hers about people wanting to go grocery shopping for seniors, Facebook groups being set up as a way to connect with elderly neighbors who needed help while being quarantined. The response was overwhelming and steadfast. It reinforced my belief that kindness is contagious. Rebecca says she is so grateful to be a small part of something that inspired so many others to want to help their neighbors, reach out to their community, or just call their own parents or grandparents.

"This is a tough time for everyone, no matter who you are, so I feel like the more we can do to help those who are struggling the most, the better off we're going to be at the end of this, whenever it's over."

I ask Rebecca if she comes from a family where her parents instilled kindness and doing the right thing. She doesn't hesitate and brings up her dad, who is from India. At Christmastime, he would go around and chat with homeless people, buying them a coffee or giving them a small gift. Growing up in a place where slums were sometimes right next to wealthy homes, he developed a respect for people living around him, no matter what socioeconomic class they were in.

"I feel like hearing about my dad's experience and growing up in Los Angeles, I do believe he instilled that notion to help people. And yeah, I guess I'm really lucky for that. But I'm also surrounded by, I have to say, a lot of really good people who would have done the exact same thing."

I tell her: "Your dad must be so proud of you."

"My dad, he's funny. I sent him what I wrote on Twitter right after this happened, before it made the news, and I said, 'Hey, this is what happened.' And my dad is not a very emotional person, [but] he said he teared up a little bit. At the same time, like I said, so many people would have done the same thing, it just was . . ." She pauses. "I was in the right place."

I ask about some of the messages she's received since posting her grocery store run for a stranger. "Was there anything that struck you when you read other people's reactions that made you emotional or had an impact on what that story did for someone else?"

Her response makes me cry: "I think one that stood out to me the most was a firefighter that was there on 9/11, who lost a lot of his comrades fighting the fires at the Twin Towers. And he sent me a message, telling me about his family, and he just thanked me for what I did. I felt like I didn't deserve a message from a 9/11 firefighter. What I did was not even close to the level that he did of public service."

Rebecca also says those who reached out and asked for help made her feel like this was bigger than the moment of buying a stranger's groceries. "I felt like I was bridging these gaps for people and helping them to connect with each other on how to get elderly people groceries, or immunocompromised people the medications that they need, so they don't have to go out of their house, and that was really special."

In a follow-up tweet a few days after she sent the viral message, Rebecca thanked everyone who shared her story. She reinforced her belief that she isn't anyone that special. "Most people I know would have done the same thing I did. I was just in the right place at the right time." She added, "I think that this was just kind of a small light in a dark time, like a nice story of kindness that inspired a lot of people. I'm grateful for that."

Mr. Rogers's words of wisdom—"Look for the helpers"—has never been more true. It's not just about being kind. It's about making a connection with others. We aren't generous out of selfishness, but we end being more rewarded than if we were selfish. We need those connections like we need air and water, but it's hard to find each other in times like these.

Mr. Rogers was smart to tell us to look for the helpers. But Rebecca's example made others want to be the helpers, too.

Chapter 18

SHARE YOUR SMILE MOVEMENT

A wise person once said, Today, give someone else a smile. It might be the only sunshine they see all day.

I thought of that quote when I read the story about Robertino Rodriguez, a respiratory therapist from San Diego. He posted a photo of himself on Instagram during the height of the coronavirus pandemic, dressed head to toe in his PPE (personal protective equipment). But what was noticeably different about him was he had pinned on a laminated picture of himself smiling, so people could see what he looked like.

He wrote: "I felt bad for my patients in ER when I would come in the room with my face covered in PPE. A reassuring smile makes a big difference to a scared patient."

The picture was shared thousands of times over, and health care workers from around the world were doing the same thing, sharing their pictures on their PPE. It became the "Share Your Smile" movement. Robertino says he never thought a small idea would have such a huge impact on the world.

I talked to Robertino in April on one of his rare days off. We did our interview on Skype, and I found that he's the same warm person I expected after reading about his wonderful story on social media.

I start off by asking how he's doing. I can tell he's tired, but he's one of those people who just keeps going regardless of how he's feeling.

"It's been just busy, just a lot of patients keep coming in. They're staying just a lot longer on the ventilator than they were before. Within a week or two, they're usually a lot better, but these days people are staying on the vent for a month or longer, so it's just been . . . a lot of work. It takes a team effort really to work with just one patient, so you have to work a lot. It's just a little more tiring, more consuming, than ever before."

Robertino explains what a respiratory therapist does: He works with patients who have cardiopulmonary, or heart and lung, issues. A lot of the patients he's seen with COVID-19 have the virus attacking their lungs. For patients who are unable to breathe on their own, this machine is used to provide oxygen. His job is to manage the ventilators and all the changes on the ventilators. Part of his job is to make sure the patient's airway is protected. A tube keeps the patient breathing, and it has to always be there, secure. Sometimes Robertino has to move the patients from side to side so that no pressure ulcers develop from bony prominences (bones underneath the skin can cause pressure ulcers). When he does the turns, the tube has to be maneuvered so it's not kinked or compromised in any way. Basically, every patient who has COVID is his patient.

Before the pandemic happened, Robertino worked in level-one trauma and was always busy, but the difference is patients would normally get better fairly quickly and would go home within a certain amount of time. Now they are staying a lot longer with more complicated issues.

I ask Robertino how he came up with the simple idea of putting a picture on his uniform. He says it started when they had to begin wearing masks all the time.

"I've been at the same hospital for eleven years. I used to be an ER tech before I started as a respiratory therapist. I've known many of these people for a long time, but now when you're wearing a scrub cap on your head, all you see is eyes. A lot of times, I don't know who's who, and you start to lose that connection with people you've always known. People now aren't hugging or shaking hands, so sometimes I would see coworkers, and I wouldn't know who they were because they were all suited and masked up. I felt we were losing that connection to people I knew."

He would go in to see his patients, and instead of seeing him smile and introduce himself, he realized, they were meeting someone who was unrecognizable. "They would just see eyes as I tried to introduce myself, and not be able to see me smiling."

He felt bad about that. How they must feel, lying in a hospital bed, scared because they weren't allowed visitors. Totally alone. And it bothered him all the time.

"The next day, when I came in, I remembered we had a laminator machine in our break room, and I first thought about making my work badge that has a little picture of me on it bigger. But then I'm like, 'Let me put a big picture of me where I'm smiling, put my name and my title, what I do.'"

That's how the idea came to him, Robertino says—he just put himself in their shoes, looking up at someone and not being able to see a smile. Just a mask. No lips moving as he's trying to say hello or see how they are. After he put the picture of himself on his chest, he walked down the halls of the hospital, and everyone told him they wanted to do the same. His patients loved it.

"As soon as they saw me, they'd either laugh or just have a big smile on their face. I could see it. They were just so happy that they could see my face behind the mask." He told them: "You know, right now, I'm smiling at you, too, just like in this photo." For a few moments, they forgot how scared they were.

Once he posted his picture on Instagram, it was shared by thousands. People loved it. "It was so fast. I did it on a Saturday, and then the next day, I wake up to my Instagram, and it's just flooded with messages. And then more and more doctors and nurses started doing it, and it was amazing. I saw pictures from Africa, Brazil, Germany, Ireland, that they were also doing it, and it was just a small idea that caught on."

Robertino says it wasn't just for the patients; it made him feel better, too. He says he got into the field of work because he likes to take care of others. What he's doing with his smiling badge is helping him connect with his patients, and that in turn makes him happier as well.

I ask if Robertino has always had a connection to people like this—do his patients feel comfortable with him? He says this is who he is. He's always wanted to help people. That's why he chose the medical field. The start of the pandemic was terrible, because not only was it making people sick, but it was also making it hard for him to connect with his patients. They couldn't see him or his smile.

"People have said they aren't surprised this idea came from me. That's just something I want to keep happening despite the time we're in."

Robertino says he gets his sunny disposition from his family. They are all close, naturally and geographically. "My grandparents live half a block from my sister, the next block is my mom and my brother. We all live within a one-block radius."

He tells me his mom is a preschool teacher, and his dad teaches English as a second language. "I think it came from them. That is the way I was raised, like, 'Always take care of people. Be good to people.' And it's also in you, too. You have to have it yourself."

I ask Robertino if he remembers a specific patient who made a big impact on him once he decided to put his smiling face on his PPE. He smiles and tells me about one particular man who comes to the hospital a lot and didn't recognize Robertino because of all his clothing and masks. When he saw the smiling badge on the PPE, he started laughing. "Oh, Robertino," he said. "And I was like, 'Yeah, it's me.' He's like, 'Without that, I wouldn't have known it was you because you were covered up.'" His patient has problems with asthma and chronic obstructive pulmonary disease (COPD). Despite all the health issues, Robertino says, he's always laughing. But during this moment, the man was scared because he had a fever and thought he might have COVID.

"Thankfully, it was a negative test, but he was scared. So that's the one I do remember, with that patient I worked with many times before. He was happy when he found out it was me underneath my mask and hospital uniform."

I ask Robertino what he thinks will happen after this is all over: "Will we come out of this better, stronger, with better empathy for each other or more of a connection to our families?"

He says, "I hope when we do, and we're back to whatever the new normal is, that people remember how much empathy people had for each other during this, how good it would be if everybody continued to help each other out. And that people will remember how to just be so kind as we were during all this time. I hope people connect more and are more inclined to being just more empathetic to everybody else around them."

I tell him that's what I hope, too, and I'm by nature an optimistic person, but this time has been tough for even the sunniest of personalities.

"I mean, you never know what happens after things go back to normal. But I hope that everybody else remembers the good thing, like helping the neighbor out, kind of, going forward. And even though we see people and they're strangers, I hope now more people are like, 'We went through this together.'"

Robertino says he hopes people also remember how important it is to engage with one another and how little things like a "hello" or "how are you" or just a smile walking down the street, those little things, how much they can mean when you don't have them anymore.

"I definitely miss those people I see, who would always give each other a hug, and now we can't. It's that little thing that would be normal, and now you miss it so much. All of those little things mean more than all the bigger things that people think are so important—the material things. It's the small things that mean so much when you don't have them anymore."

I tell Robertino that my whole way of life has changed because I love to hug people. Even strangers. When I'm out doing weather on television, that's my whole reason of being there, other than doing a weather forecast—it's to connect with people. Shaking hands, hugging. It's going to be difficult not being able to share that kind of human contact. He says he's a big hugger, too, and hugs really do help.

"They relieve stress, and they have that connection with people, and not having it now, it's sad. I hope people remember, it's all those little things that really mean the most [more] than anything else."

Even if you make that snap decision to become a helper, even if there's an adrenaline rush that lasts for days as the kindness spreads across the globe, there is an after. You have to figure out where you go next. In the movies, the superhero saves the day, and the credits roll. The regular heroes still have to go to work the next day.

I ask Robertino what keeps him going. The type of job he's in has to be so high-stress along with being physically and emotionally difficult.

"What keeps me going is I just want be there to help my patients and help my colleagues. I feel bad today because they called me earlier.

They didn't have enough staff, but I just couldn't do it today. I did eight days straight, my legs were just . . . I needed a day today to just catch up on rest, rest my legs."

He explains when the hospital is short-staffed, that means patients get less attention. He ends up doing double the work, and he's giving less time to his patients. And that makes him feel bad. "And my colleagues. They're overworked, too. It's very stressful. That's what keeps me going, though. Helping colleagues and helping my patients." Robertino says he's also supposed to be off tomorrow, but he's going back in.

I ask if his family is worried about him. He says definitely. But he can't stop now. Too many people are relying on him. I ask if he's always wanted to be in the medical profession. He laughs and says he grew up with parents who were teachers. At the beginning, he was studying history, to be a college professor, but he didn't feel it was a calling. When he dated a girl who became a paramedic, that was when the lightbulb went off, and he knew it was what he wanted to do.

"I became an EMT, and then from there it took off. I got a job in the hospital, and I had a friend who had finished respiratory therapy school, and he started working, and I job-shadowed him and really enjoyed it. From there I went to school, and I've been doing it ever since."

I tell Robertino that his family must be so proud of him. He says yes. Growing up, there were many challenges.

"We grew up in a bad neighborhood, and I made it out. Me and my brother. He just passed the bar exam a few days ago."

Now, as Robertino's name has been in the news, his parents are even more excited about how dedicated he is to his job and his patients.

I ask if his upbringing and the challenges his family faced gave him the attitude he has and the desire to do something. He says absolutely, and it's why he works so hard. If you want something, you have to work for it and sometimes put in even more time than others. Robertino says he grew up in a bad neighborhood without a lot of money. Now he and his brother have done something with their lives.

"When my brother passed the bar exam, I was so proud of him, so excited for him, that he did that, too. It shows to other people, if they ever ask, that you can do it, too, no matter where you come from, what neighborhood you lived in, or what circumstances you're under that you can, as long as you have a dream, you can achieve it."

It's funny how many people I talk to ascribe their kindness to the way they grew up, but they all grew up differently. It seems more like having someone show them kindness along the way opened their eyes to how much can be done with just a smile.

I ask what advice Robertino has for people getting into the profession, and how important it is to have a connection with your patients. He says always remember that your patients are people. Sometimes they can come off angry and ungrateful. It comes from a place of being in a great deal of pain. They're not at their best when he meets them—they are usually at their worst. Many are terrified.

"So, it's something you have to just remember, and as long as you treat them just like you would want to be treated, kindly, with respect, they will respond to that. And just have a lot of compassion, just to understand where they're coming from."

Robertino says he tries to put himself in his patient's shoes, asking, "What if I was that person in the bed right now, how would I feel?" He says he tries distracting patients by talking about family or what they're watching on TV, even the weather. If you just remember to treat a patient as a caring human being, you're going to be okay.

"I tell people it's one of the greatest jobs I have had. I love it, but just remember the hours are long, you do get tired, it gets difficult sometimes. Not everybody can handle the job."

Robertino says he wouldn't change it for the world, even what he's going through right now in a pandemic. He's thankful he has a job and knows that many people have jobs that they hate. He recommends that anyone who wants to go into the medical field start off job-shadowing or being a volunteer. "Many people say they want to be a pediatric nurse because they love babies. And I tell them you need to volunteer first. Those babies are very sick. They are crying. Some don't make it. Some of your patients you will see from the beginning, and you will know them until their last breath. You have a compassionate heart, that's the best thing for people who like to get in this field. But if you decide to do it, you will never regret making that decision to come do what I do."

I tell Robertino he is the definition of someone with a serving heart. He tells me his is a service industry. You have to give yourself to the people you help. To him, this is not work. You have to be compassionate and understand where others are coming from in the worst moment of their life sometimes. No one wants to be in the hospital. You have to remember that. Be aware of that.

He says there's a healing aspect besides medicine. "Just your presence being there, being joyful with them and nice to them, makes a big difference. And the mental health is important here with them, too, when you're making them smile and laugh . . . that also helps them heal."

I tell him I've read up on all the studies that prove there are endorphins when you're happy, smiling, and laughing. Making sunshine.

"Yes, exactly. That's the same thing I tell people. Like the big picture badge I wear. Help people to smile and to laugh and be happy. It all helps mentally. It helps you heal. If you're sad, depressed, and not connecting, your immunity can get worse. If you're nice, kind, and smiling, it makes a big, big difference."

Robertino smiles. I smile back. And for a moment, I feel our sunshine filling up the room.

Chapter 19

TEBOW
(MAKES THE DASH SPECIAL)

I started this book with one rule: no celebrities or heralded philanthropists. I wanted to focus on everyday people doing kind things for others. Football player J. J. Watt made headlines for his charity work in Texas and the millions of dollars he raised after Hurricane Harvey. Dolly Parton is constantly making good-news stories with her foundations, especially her initiative of getting kids to read. She's given away millions of books to children around the world. I love what Gary Sinise has done with his celebrity for those who sacrifice on our behalf: active duty, veterans, first responders, and their loved ones. These stars are all wonderful and deserve to have a spotlight on the charity work they do, but I wanted the book reserved for regular people.

The thing is, I do know a regular person who is relentless in his drive to help others, but this regular guy just happened to be famous. When I met Tim Tebow to talk about his foundation and how he wants to help others, I left that interview a better person. This book wouldn't be as good without his story.

Tim Tebow is well known in the sports world as a Heisman Trophy winner, a former NFL quarterback, and a professional baseball player. Long before he became famous, he spent his early years in the Philippines, where his parents served as missionaries. He has used his platform to do incredible things for others with his Tim Tebow Foundation and has followed his family's mission to promote faith and help those less fortunate all over the world.

Tebow believes he has been given this moment to help others. In the months that have gone by since I sat down with him to talk about why he's here on earth, I've come to believe he's one of the most authentic, giving people I've ever met. When people ask me some of my favorite people I've ever interviewed or met, Tim Tebow is at the top of my list.

When we meet, I ask first about his early years and experiences overseas with his parents, which he believes are the foundation for his serving heart. One of his favorite sayings is: "If you want to impact the world, impact people." Tim says his parents instilled the importance of God's word and the responsibility that we have to give back to others. That was passed on to him: the desire to make a difference in people's lives.

Tim says the moment that shaped him and his vision for helping others happened when he was fifteen and he and his family were in a village where he met a boy named Sherwin. Sherwin was born with his feet on backward and was viewed as "cursed" in his small community. Those around him looked at Sherwin as less significant because of his deformity. He wasn't allowed to be a part of the tribe and was treated terribly. But for Tim, being able to hold that boy, who was a child of God like everyone else despite differences, made him realize that his biggest wish was to help others.

"I knew leaving that village that day that I wanted to fight for people like this young boy. That was more important than any sport

I would ever play. I wanted to have a life that mattered, and really, I wanted to have a life to fight for people who couldn't fight for themselves."

The mission statement of the Tim Tebow Foundation is "to bring faith, hope, and love to those needing a brighter day in their darkest hour of need." Tim says he wrote that, thinking about the young boy he met that day, as well as all the boys and girls around the world who need us to fight for them. He says he'll continue to do it as long as he's here on earth.

I mention that when you meet kids like Sherwin, that's when you realize how blessed we truly are, and some of our problems and challenges are small in comparison.

Tim says he tries to encourage young people to go on mission trips, no matter what their background or faith is, and to try and see the world outside of America. That's not to minimize what people are going through here, but to give more perspective about what others are dealing with; then maybe being thankful will mean something different because of those experiences beyond your own backyard. To go overseas, he says, where his parents and sister lived for a long time, and to see what others are dealing with—just hoping one day for some food to eat—is eye-opening.

When Tim was visiting Thailand, he served meals to those less fortunate. He saw lines so long that he knew there were people who weren't going to eat that day. They were going to run out of food. If that doesn't impact someone, then he doesn't know what will. He wants people to realize that, not to be disappointed but to know how truly blessed you are and what to be grateful for in life. What makes the difference, though, isn't hearing about the hungry or even seeing them with your own eyes. It's helping them get food that day and knowing your life has more value when you are valuing the lives of others.

Tim says his parents are his biggest role models and that watching them give so much of their lives to help others is what drives him. They give back to people who can never do anything for them, without any benefit except feeling like they are doing what they were put on this earth to do: serve others. That's what real love looks like.

"Choosing the best interests of another person and acting on their behalf. Sometimes people get caught up in 'How do we do that?' instead of just doing something—anything—like holding a deformed child to show others around them he deserves love as much as any of us do."

He says it starts and ends with people, because people matter most. That's a big part of his faith. "Love the Lord your God with all your heart and with all your soul and with all your strength and with all your mind, and Love your neighbor as yourself."

We get so caught up in rules, Tim says, but if you really want to have a life of significance, you're going to have a life that impacts people. You have to ask yourself: What would be a life of significance? For many, that means money, fame, and power. For Tim, a life of significance is measured by the lives that you change, not the dollars you make. "It's important to realize that a life of significance isn't about what we have, but what we give."

I follow Tim on social media, and before the interview, I saw a selfie he did with prisoners at a jail in Texas. He was smiling, and the guys in their prison uniforms were smiling back. I bring up the picture and the prison visits that he does on a regular basis. He says visiting prisoners is honestly one of his favorite things to do, especially those on death row or in a maximum-security prison, because "you're going to see guys that can never do anything for you."

He loves doing it because so much of the world has written them off. Life has literally locked them up and thrown away the key. But just because they might have done some bad things in their past doesn't mean that they don't have any more value left.

"Because they do, they have value to God, and they have value to me, and I want to go in there and truly love these men, share and care for them, and be able to let them know that I just want to come here and hang with you and entertain you, but more than anything, I want to share hope with you. I care about you. And there's nothing that I want from you except to be able to give you hope, even in this tough time in your life."

I have tears in my eyes after tells me about the prisoners. Then I think about forgiveness. What does it mean to him?

"We ask for forgiveness when we realize that we've messed up or we've done something wrong. When you realize the depths of our own depravity, then it makes grace that much more special. It makes God's grace and what He did on the cross that much more special."

Tim Tebow says his legacy is going to be fighting for people who can't fight for themselves. In every way possible. His foundation helps kids who can't afford hospitals, and volunteers bring the children in to be cared for from all over the world. They help take care of orphans in six different countries. There's a wish-granting organization for kids with life-threatening illnesses. There are a lot of initiatives where he wants to make as big a difference as humanly possible.

"I could sit here and tell story after story of the kid that was thrown away or abandoned or thrown into a wall or tied up and in chains. We just had a young boy that passed away because he had special needs and his family refused to give him medical attention. It's important that we fight for these kids, because they need us, and they need us to be a voice for them."

Even when he's talking about sports, Tim reflects on his values and his upbringing. At a press conference during his journey in baseball with the New York Mets, he was asked about doubting himself. Here's his response that went viral on social media: "Yeah, of course. It'd be a lie to say no. I think it's: What do you do with that doubt? What do you do with the uncertainty? What do you do when you feel like you're struggling with something? I think that's important, because I think we all have that in our lives at places and times when we're going through things. And ultimately, in a lot more important situations than sports."

Tim says you have to ask yourself: Why are you doing this? Are you having fun? Do you love it? Then have a mindset to continue what you're doing so you don't let the doubt or uncertainty control your mind and mentality.

"There's a lot of things in life that you get thrown into where you're uncertain, but I think that's where faith and determination and perseverance really come into play—not when things are going really well."

Tebow signed a minor-league deal with the Mets in 2016, and he still hasn't reached the majors. But that doesn't matter to him. He says it's not the focus of his life. He has bigger things that keep him busy.

One of my favorite programs of his foundation is his "Night to Shine" evening. The premise is to give kids with special needs a prom night. Just to see those kids all dressed up, grinning from ear to ear, dancing, and getting their pictures taken all together having a good time. In February 2020, more than seven hundred churches worldwide took part, and 110,000 guests were honored. Tim took part in Tallahassee, Florida, and shared pictures and videos from his evening on social media.

I ask him how he juggles all of this—sports, family, and his foundation. He says he dedicates time and energy to what matters most. If it doesn't matter, he doesn't worry about it. But he goes all in when he pursues something. "I feel like one of the biggest tragedies in life is when you look back and you were successful at something that really doesn't matter. And I don't want to do that. I want to go after things that really matter."

If you're still wondering whether Tim Tebow is the real deal, there are snippets of him all over the Internet doing good things when no one is looking.

From a 2009 *GQ* article:

I ran into Tebow one time, out on the sidewalk. He was with all his friends, and I asked him if I could take a picture with him. But my batteries died. I said I had some batteries in my truck, can you wait here? He said, Yeah, no problem. I came back ten minutes later. He was sitting here, by himself, waiting for me to take a picture. Any other person would have just left with their friends. . . . Then he offered me his number so when I got it developed he could autograph it. That's Tim Tebow.

From ESPN in 2012:

When the world was pulling its hair out in the hour after Tebow had stunned the Pittsburgh Steelers with an 80-yard OT touchdown pass to Demaryius Thomas in the playoffs? Twitter was exploding with 9,420 tweets about Tebow per second? When an ESPN poll was naming him the most popular athlete in America? Well, Tebow was spending that hour talking to 16-year-old Bailey Knaub about her 73 surgeries so far and what TV shows she likes!

Bailey's mom, Kathy, from Loveland, Colorado, couldn't believe that Tim Tebow was talking to her daughter: "Here he'd just played the game of his life, and the first thing he does after his press conference is come find Bailey and ask, 'Did you get anything to eat?' He acted like what he'd just done wasn't anything, like it was all about Bailey."

After the Pulse nightclub shooting in Orlando, Florida, Tebow went and visited the victims, including a former high school football teammate, Rodney Sumter, a bartender who was shot three times. Rodney said that his friend had always been an awesome person. But it wasn't just Rodney Tim wanted to see. He wanted to see all the victims, and that's what he did.

I've read articles about Tim paying off layaway orders at Christmas and visiting people in hospitals after surgeries.

I have heard the story of Tim seeing someone having a seizure at an Arizona Fall League game. He went over and talked to the man who had fallen to make sure he was okay.

Stories of Tim Tebow the kindhearted do-gooder are everywhere. And that's why I decided to break my rule about not having any celebrities in this book. Because making sunshine is what Tim Tebow does.

A quote from the 2009 GQ article sums up Tim Tebow very well:

When you die, there's gonna be a tombstone, and on that tombstone there's gonna be a name, and there's gonna be a date. And for me, it's going to be 1987, and then it's gonna have a dash . . . I want that dash to mean something. I want that dash to be special. I want that dash to represent that Tim Tebow finished strong. And, most importantly, when I get to heaven, I want Jesus to say, well done, my good and faithful servant.

According to Tim, once you've successfully served others, the only reasonable next step is to find more people to serve.

Chapter 20

OFFICER CONLEY

There's an annual event that started back in 2011 in Hawthorne, California. It's called Coffee with a Cop, and the plan is simple: Police officers can meet the community in a casual way at a restaurant or coffee shop in the city they work hard to protect.

The police chief Robert Fager who came up with the idea said he was tired of "town hall" meetings and wanted an interactive way to encourage police interactions with their neighborhoods. He hoped to break down the traditional barriers that so often exist between police officers and the people they serve. The conversations are intimate and personal, important to both the residents and the officers.

I thought about the Coffee with a Cop idea when I received a message from one of my Twitter followers, Debbi Glass, after I asked for suggestions of good people out there I should feature in the book. Here is what she wrote:

> Hi Janice!
> James Madison University in Harrisonburg has an officer

named David Conley. He is affectionately known by the students as simply Conley. He literally takes the freshman student body under his wing each year and helps them by being a mentor, getting to know them, help them through hard times, and being a "parent." You can find him on Facebook by searching friends of Officer Conley at JMU. Go to any JMU football game and if he is there the students go crazy yelling Conley, Conley. He is a role model like no other I have seen and is so humble. Someone needs to tell his story. Thanks for your consideration. Good luck with your book.

For some officers, every day is meet-a-cop day. With more than twenty thousand students at JMU, there's one person whom nearly every student knows. That's him: Officer Conley.

His goal is to meet every single student, and he always takes the "good neighbor approach" when it comes to his job. "I spend a lot of time in the libraries, in the dining halls, and on campus meeting people individually. I kind of have a line that I tell everyone every year when the freshmen get here, and it's working very well."

Officer Conley has been with the James Madison University Department of Police & Public Safety since January 2005. Since then, he has become an ambassador from the police department to JMU. He even has his own Facebook page: "I Know Officer Conley at JMU." There are more than 2,500 members registered.

Over the last decade and a half, Officer Conley has met easily a hundred times the number of Facebook fans he has, personally shaking students' hands and asking how he can help them. Whether it's eating lunch with the kids at various dining areas, taking part in school safety programs, or being an escort for tours on campus for future students and their parents, he takes the time and makes an effort to make a difference.

"The only thing that changes in this is the amount of years that I've been here. I just started my fifteenth year, and I'm trying to get around and meet every single person, to help my students any way that I can."

He tells his students there are "twenty thousand of you guys and one me. So, I'm going to ask that when you see me, you take a minute to come and reintroduce yourself. It gives me a chance, an opportunity, to learn your name and who you are."

When I start talking to him, I know immediately that Officer Conley is indeed the real deal. He tells me all of the kids know him as Conley. No "Officer." No "sir." No "mister."

How does he make it look so easy? Conley says he's always done his job differently, and it's because he didn't like the interactions he was seeing from law enforcement in his own neighborhood, growing up. Here's how it began: His uncle leased a gas station in Shenandoah, and he and his friends hung out in the back of their pickup trucks. Two officers would always come by and mess with their group. "I got in an argument with a cop and told him I was smart enough to do what he did. And he kind of walked away and said, 'You're right.' We laughed. And that was on a Saturday night. I applied for a job on Monday, and about five or six weeks later, he was my training officer."

It wasn't always smooth sailing when he first began his career. There was reportedly conflict between Conley and the police chief of Elkton. According to reports, Officer Conley left the department, and the chief of police admitted to lying to get him fired. He says politics sometimes get in the way of police work. A few years later, he came to JMU. It was time for a new beginning and a different path.

Conley says tough situations arise with students, and he's aware that he needs to be a positive force for them. "It's not always about the law. It's not always about police work. It's about the compassion of helping people get through stuff."

He loves his work at JMU. I ask him if what he does is a calling. He says he doesn't look at it like that. He just says he wants to make a difference.

"Too many police officers put too much time into thinking that their job is about how many tickets they write and how many people they lock up. And a lot of administrations promote that. But when you're dealing with young people, we're trying to give them a head start in life and get them started as they grow into adults and find careers."

He says it's important to realize that young people are going to make mistakes. That's what they do, and it's how we grow. Conley admits he didn't come from one of the best backgrounds, but we can live and learn and help people the best way we can.

I ask Officer Conley if there are any stories that touched him over the years and reinforced his decision to get into this profession.

"Well, things affect you in different ways. I was working as a road deputy, and there was a domestic situation between a man and his wife and their fourteen-year-old daughter. The girl went in and shot herself in the chest because her mom and dad were arguing. That's the call that sticks with me the most throughout my career."

But for the most part, he says, he's been blessed. "I've been able to help people and save people. I was honored by JMU when they had the really bad incident at Virginia Tech."

In 2007 the tragedy at Virginia Tech left a gunman and thirty-three students dead. Local police reacted by increasing the number of training officers to deal with situations where an "active shooter" was the threat. Officer Conley was sent to Virginia Tech for three weeks and asked to walk their campus twelve hours a day, meeting as many of the students as he could: the same job he was doing at JMU, just trying to get the students back to class and feeling better. A few years later, he was contacted again and offered a job at Virginia Tech because of how well he did and his connection to the kids. He thought about it, but he didn't want to leave his community and the relationships he's built with his students. JMU acknowledged his good work and told him how much he is appreciated.

Officer Conley would like to see more police officers spending more time in the communities, getting to know residents and working with them. He knows what works when you're trying to get to know your neighbors. Conley tells me a story about a new jurisdiction that he was given in Harrisonburg: "I already knew that I was going to make it a point to go to the 7-Eleven on North Mason Street, because the minority community is over there. So, I would go to 7-Eleven every morning to get my coffee so I could be around the people that live there." He admits when he first went there, people looked at him like he was crazy, but after a few weeks of doing that, they all yelled, "Conley!" He adds, "Then I can't leave . . ." He says people don't realize how important human contact and connection really are.

I ask him how long he'll keep doing this. He says he's not sure. "I know when I leave that it's going to be really hard. It just depends on where life takes me. But I really enjoy my students right now." He tells me that's what he feels like: They are his students.

Officer Conley has made an impact on many graduating students as well. Several have gone on to pursue their own career in law enforcement.

"In Richmond, I have a friend who's a Virginia state trooper. At the beginning of football season this year, I saw the state police car pull in. A young lady get out. She came over and gave me a hug. It's not the first time I've gotten hugs from a state trooper." He laughs.

I ask Conley how he handles his celebrity status. He says he doesn't look at it that way. "James Madison University has made a positive difference in my life. We have some really good people here. What I do, or what I've done here, I'm just trying to make a difference in the world, a positive difference in my students' lives. And I have all sorts of conversations with my students. Boyfriend/girlfriend advice, what have you. They are comfortable to talk to me about anything. It's rewarding for me."

Conley tells me a story about how he was assigned to tailgates at football games. He says the first tailgate, he just talked to his students and told them that he would appreciate it if they did a few things when they took part in these activities. "One of the gentlemen students speaks up and says kindly, 'We're going to do whatever you tell us.'"

He reminded them of what they need to do to keep things safe and orderly during the tailgating parties. The entire football season, they had no issues. "Students picked up the trash before they left after the tailgate. They were respectful to each other. And I think that if more police officers would spend more time building relationships with people in the neighborhoods, we'd have less problems in our communities."

I tell Officer Conley that we need more of him and his attitude in the world today. It's not easy, doing this kind of job and investing the time and energy into it that he does on a daily basis. I tell him he's got another fan now on his Facebook page.

Before we hang up, Conley tells me how appreciative he is of our interview. He says he's going to get choked up.

"I don't look at what I do as anything special, but when I was called into a meeting and they said, 'Hey, the lady on *Fox & Friends* that writes books wants to do an interview with you,' it's . . . well, very touching for me."

I tell him he deserves the recognition. I want everyone to know about "Conley" and how he makes his own sunshine and spreads it to others. He's a wonderful example of making a difference in the world by doing a little bit every day. That's Officer Conley—approaching each day and each shift with a positive can-do attitude and a desire to help as many as he can.

Chapter 21

MORE GOOD

Mary Latham believes that once you start looking for good, you'll find it everywhere.

The last chapter in this book just happens to be about Mary, the first person I interviewed.

A photographer from New York City, Mary decided to take a journey across all fifty states to gather stories of kindness in honor of her mom, whom she lost to cancer in 2013.

I found out about Mary after talking to my friend Kelley Kramer. Kelley's mom also died of cancer, and she's always talking openly about the pain and loss of not having her mom around. Kelley is also one of the sunniest people I know at work, with a smile and a hug always ready to be given and received. When I mentioned to Kelley that I was working on a book about making sunshine, she gave me Mary's number and said: "She's one of the most amazing people I know. You have to talk to her."

I reached out to Mary, and we spoke several times on the phone.

There's no denying her sunny disposition. When we finally met in person at Fox News after her "More Good" tour was completed (pre-coronavirus), she wore a yellow sweater, and when I asked her how she was feeling, she was honest (while smiling) and said: "Tired, relieved, and a little overwhelmed."

When we began our conversation about her time on the road in her mom's Subaru, she lit up the studio. This was her making sunshine after a very dark time in her life.

The idea for finding "More Good" came to her after talking to her mom, Patricia Latham, on the morning of the 2012 Sandy Hook Elementary School shooting in Newtown, Connecticut. One of our worst shootings in history, that horrific event took the lives of twenty children and six teachers. Mary was working at a law office in Manhattan when the news broke, and she couldn't stop reading the latest information about the tragic events. It was so unimaginable and so evil. "How could something like this happen at a school?" she kept asking herself. "To little children?" Overwhelming sickness and dread were overtaking her, but she couldn't take her eyes off the unfolding horror story.

While Mary was watching the tragic, hellish headlines unfold on social media and online, she was momentarily distracted by a coworker who came by. Mary says he clearly had no idea what was happening in the awful, dark world around him; he was just so excited about the coffee that a complete stranger had bought him and several others in line for no reason. When he was about to pay, the barista told him that a man had been in earlier, buying gift cards for employees. He had purchased one for himself, given the barista a hundred dollars, and asked them to run it out on all the customers in line.

Mary told me that her free-coffee coworker was going through several challenges at the time, with a marital separation, a parent who had passed away, and a back surgery on the horizon. It was a pretty bad year for him, but that free coffee had put a smile on his face and a spring in his step. She says she'll never forget his joyfulness juxtaposed with the real-life nightmare happening simultaneously.

Still distraught and needing someone to talk to, Mary called her mom to talk about what she was witnessing in the news. At the time, Patricia was going through her second round of cancer. She had beat it the first time and was determined to do it again. Mary started the conversation, trying to be upbeat, by telling her mom about the coworker and the free coffee. She didn't want to weigh her mom down with the shooting tragedy, but suddenly, she couldn't help it. (Something I've learned over the years is: You're never too old to need your mother.)

How were these parents, teachers, students, and friends going to get over a day like this? Mary asked her mother, crying. She insisted that evil had taken over the world.

Patricia listened quietly and agreed with how terrible and evil the Sandy Hook shooting was. Of course it was heartbreaking and absolutely tragic. And then she politely interrupted Mary and said: "Mary, you've got to focus on that coffee story, like what a cool thing that guy would do that. There'll always be tragedies and terrible things that will happen in our lives, it's inevitable, but still there's more good out there, you just have to look for it.'"

She wanted her daughter to focus on the goodness left in the world. Because there is so much of that, too. You just have to be willing to choose hope and happiness and keep your eyes open for them. The advice stuck with Mary that day and through the years to come.

Mary first began her search for good with "The GrAttitude Project," a Facebook page asking readers to submit stories of kindness. She wanted to hear about people doing wonderful things for others to get her through a tough time. It wasn't long after she began that website that her mom went in for surgery.

A week later, her mom passed away. Instead of being overcome with grief, Mary wanted to focus on the good. Just like her mom had told her to do. And it made her drive for finding it even bigger.

"I decided that when I was ready, I was going to pack up her car and literally drive to every state in the country and look for the good that's out there, meet these people, and document the journey."

That was in 2013. Three years later, on October 29, 2016, Mary Latham hit the road in "Old Blue," her mom's Subaru, and made some T-shirts to hand out to anyone who helped her along her journey. She called it "More Good."

I called Mary before she completed her trip across America; she would wrap it up right before Thanksgiving.

I teared up when she told me about some of the amazing strangers she was meeting. Mary heard my voice break and confessed that she had been crying for three years straight, but they've been mostly happy tears upon hearing other people's stories, or staying in the homes of strangers who heard about her project and offered to take her in as she worked to complete it.

One story she told me has become a favorite of hers, and now mine. A bank teller in Rhode Island remembered a bad day at work that was turned around by just a thoughtful treat.

Mary explains: "This happened years ago to this woman. But she still remembers it. She was having a really bad day, and I guess it was visible on her face, because a total stranger came into the bank and looked at her and could sense something was wrong. The customer asked, 'Are you okay? Is there anything I can do for you?' The woman said she was embarrassed at the time. She was, like, in her twenties. And she's just like, 'Oh, no, no, no, no, nothing. Nothing that some peanut M&M's won't fix!'"

And thirty minutes later, wouldn't you know that same customer came back in and slid a bag of peanut M&M's under the window to the teller, and she never forgot it.

"She told her kids and her grandkids, and it's now thirty years later that she's telling me this story. I think about that a lot. Was she going through a bad breakup? Was she hurt? I never found out. But those M&M's changed her day."

I tell her I'm reminded of the Winnie-the-Pooh quote by A. A. Milne: "Sometimes the smallest things take up the most room in your heart." Mary agrees, and adds:

"People are getting diagnosed with cancer or they're losing an uncle in a car crash or whatever is happening in the world, it's important to just pay attention to the people around us and do these small little acts or just smile at each other, you know, tiny little things that we can do to kind of put that positive out there."

Mary says that's the main idea of her More Good trip. Some people think that an act of kindness has to be a really large, grand act, and there are certainly people doing that—donating kidneys to strangers, paying for neighbors to go to college. There are amazing things going on in the world, but people can get overwhelmed by that idea. It truly does mean that sometimes it's just the little things that mean the most.

At a time when political news takes up so much of the oxygen around us, Mary tells me, she never discussed politics with the people she stayed with or interviewed. She found that who someone voted for simply doesn't matter. For her, there is just one thing that stood out, and it's a thread common to everyone she met: "They're all good people who want to be a part of something that helps others."

Mary learned on her trip that the "More Good" is happening all around us, just like her mom said it would be. We just have to look for it.

I agree that's part of it, but something I've learned over the years is you have to open your heart to it, too. If you reward people for being generous, you get more of that. If you reward someone for being a grouch, you get more of that, too. Imagine a world where we rewarded only the forward-looking, generous behavior. You have to acknowledge and be grateful for those little things that can change your mood AND your attitude: a wave from a neighbor or a smile of encouragement when you need it the most. But you have to be open to it and look for it.

"I think some people always feel like once you put yourself in that corner of, well, nothing good ever happens to me—well, then that's going to follow you. But if you can't find something good happening to you, then YOU can try to be that good for someone else. It's a choice, and it's action."

I ask her about the people she met who have dealt with a tragedy and are trying to put that loss into something good, like the families of the Sandy Hook children who were taken from us that day. The ones who have lost the most are sometimes the most generous, kind, and giving people. They became strong in their grief and want to turn that sadness into goodness. "Kind of like your mom dying of cancer and you making something positive out of it to keep her spirit alive." Mary says a lot of the stories are like that—people trying to do better for others after something terrible happens.

I ask Mary if she thinks about her mom when she looks back at her incredible journey. She admits that she thinks about her all the time. Mary's mother was her biggest fan. Always positive and relentlessly optimistic. She smiled despite being sick; she didn't want to scare her kids. And that attitude, it radiated from her.

"Like sunshine," I say.

Mary smiles. She remembers a quote she heard at the beginning of her journey, and it took a while to process it. "It's when you lose someone that you love, it shatters your heart into a million pieces. But all the cracks let so much more light in."

She misses her mom every day and wishes she could have a glass of wine, play some Scrabble, or just talk on the phone with her. It's a bittersweet feeling, though, because if her mom hadn't died, Mary never would have done this big thing. She's had so many amazing experiences, and there's been so much sunlight after darkness.

"I think we just go through life in this robotic fashion, and we take the light for granted. But you hit that darkness of grief, and you're grasping for any flicker of light. And you see it and appreciate it much more."

"It makes you grateful," I say.

Just like her mom, Patricia, told her daughter, Mary, that terrible day at Sandy Hook.

"My mother had told me that there's always going to be tragedies and horrible things that will happen in our lives and in the world, but that there would always be more good out there—if you look for it."

All of this happened because on December 14, on a day that was full of sadness, another person instead did something kind by buying someone a free coffee. That was the moment Mary's journey began. And Mary says:

"Anyone at any time could be that person. The one that causes the spark that changes an entire life."

EPILOGUE

I was recently going through some old texts from early March, when we were at the beginning of the pandemic. My good friend Jen, whom I met when I was first diagnosed with MS (she was my doctor's nurse practitioner, and we became good friends over the last fifteen years), was sending me some practical advice and words of encouragement. Because I'm compromised, with a neurological disease, and considered more at risk for contracting the coronavirus, Jen was helping me overcome some of my fears and anxiety.

She wrote: "There will be loss, tragedy, and it will push us mentally, spiritually, and perhaps even physically, but resilience is only developed through adversity. I choose hope."

These words came before my husband lost both of his parents to COVID-19. We were unaware of the tragedy and devastating loss that was about to unfold for our family.

I remember reading her beautiful words and feeling better, almost taking a big deep breath and exhaling. One text, a few kind words, can help get you through a tough moment.

Though it was a time when we were forced to be distant from each other, in many ways, it brought me closer to people than ever before, many of them complete strangers.

My assistant, Isabelle, who helped arrange many of the interviews in this book, asked me if I wanted to take a break from writing and doing Skype interviews after my husband's parents died. I told her I didn't want to. These connections with others were helping me feel better. There were a few times during my back-and-forth with the wonderful people you've met in these pages when I shared what had happened to my in-laws. I felt closer to these people, strangely, than to friends I've had for twenty-five years.

Carrie, the mom whose daughter has diabetes and who had that beautiful moment with the FedEx driver sanitizing her package, sent me thoughtful texts after our interview. One day she asked if her brother-in-law, Frankie, could perform a magic show for my kids via Zoom. She told me he was doing these for family members and friends, and that it was a wonderful distraction and perhaps a moment when Sean and I could take a break and let someone else take over and entertain Matthew and Theodore. We arranged a time, and for forty-five minutes, Frankie performed magic tricks via video chat. My kids laughed and were mesmerized as they watched the show from their tablet. Sean and I poured a glass of wine and watched them from a distance enjoying the virtual magic show. We will never forget that moment during the pandemic when grief and sadness were replaced with joy and wonder for our children. That experience happened because of Carrie. And Carrie happened because I was trying to find stories of sunshine for this book. It caused a ripple effect of kindness and light.

Talking to all these special people—many who had gone through loss and challenges of their own—brought me strength and helped me find wings I never knew I had.

It also helped me realize the strength I had all around me. Family and friends were certainly always a phone call or FaceTime away, but there were surprising, uplifting moments like the neighborhood firefighter who brought us dinner one evening and left it on the doorstep, or when the principal at our kids' school called unexpectedly just to check in and see if there was anything she could do.

The day I went back into the office at Fox to pick up some clothes (I was running out of "TV" outfits, doing weather from home), I was greeted by stacks of unopened cards from viewers on my desk. There were dozens of beautifully written letters and prayer cards. Such inspiring words that comforted me and my family. I was overwhelmed with gratitude. I recognized that sunshine was being sent our way. Just like Gerard and his birthday cards from strangers.

These pages you're holding gave me hope during a time that was incredibly dark and challenging. Making a book about making sunshine lifted me up and got me through days that were filled with sadness, and reminded me, like my friend Jen wrote in her text, that I can choose hope.

I look back and I believe this book was meant to be written. It was fate that put it out into the universe, not just to share these beautiful stories of human beings being nice to each other, but to help me and my family realize that there is goodness and kindness all around us. Like my friend Mary Latham says, "You just have to look for it."

At the beginning of this book, I told you about my pandemic-canceled plans to go to Vegas for my fiftieth birthday. How my thoughtful husband planned the most amazing celebration despite the challenges that we were all living and dealing with.

But I saved the story to tell you about my greatest birthday gift.

I haven't owned a bike in forty years. I borrowed one about five years ago, when my family visited our friends on Long Beach Island, and what they say is true—the skill came back pretty quickly, and once I got my balance again, I was pedaling like I did back when I was ten years old.

When the pandemic hit and we were quarantined, I saw the whole neighborhood coming to life with bikes and families. My youngest son, Theodore, had not yet learned how to ride. He was very nervous every time we tried to teach him. We didn't force it, because we've learned that Teddy is someone who has to be ready to try something new. Perhaps there was something about seeing everyone out on their bikes. Suddenly, there was more time to try, try again!

One day Theodore announced to us: "I'll be brave today." Meaning that this was the day he would push forward and get on that bike again.

My husband took him out by himself so he didn't have the pressure of his mom and brother watching. In just a few minutes I heard the words: "I did it! I did it!" And lo and behold, my sweet boy was riding his bike. My husband caught it on video, and I was able to witness it myself a few minutes later. There's something very special about those first few pedals of freedom. As my husband told Teddy: "Now that you know how to ride a bike, you can never unlearn it. You'll know how to ride a bike for the rest of your life."

It was perhaps in that moment that I realized I, too, wanted a bike. Not just so I could remember that feeling of freedom from when I was a child first learning how to ride—I now wanted to do this as a family.

Wanting a bike was one thing. Finding one during a pandemic was no small feat. New bikes were practically extinct. I ended up borrowing one from our friends before the one Sean bought finally arrived six weeks later, and he had to drive to another state to pick it up.

So why am I telling you this story? Because one of my favorite days of my life was the day I took a bike ride with my family around the neighborhood during the pandemic. Sean packed a little snack of cookies and water. He brought a ball for us to kick around, and we took a fifteen-minute ride to a little patch of grass with some trees one town over. We parked our bikes, took off our helmets, and opened up the picnic blanket.

It was a reminder that the simplest, most satisfying things in life can't be bought. I remember lying down on the grass, looking up through the tree branches and the tapestry of leaves, seeing the beams of sunlight peeking through.

And I was happy.

ACKNOWLEDGMENTS

Several years ago, Fox News Radio came to me asking if I could come up with an idea for a minute-long segment that would air between commercials. I was already recording a weather forecast each day, but this would be something additional that could be used as "filler" (time that needed to be filled during the various hours of the day). My broadcasting background began in radio, and even though I do love what I do on television, there's something very special about the spoken word. Sometimes listening to (or reading) stories, as opposed to seeing them on a screen, is in many ways more effective. I find you retain or absorb the information better as opposed to sometimes getting distracted by video or what the anchor who is delivering the story looks like. For example, if my mom hears me reporting on the radio, she will comment on the content of the information. She will say, "Oh, I loved the one about the man that goes to visit his mom and brings her flowers every day." When Stella sees me on TV, while I'm sure she appreciates the message I'm trying to convey, more often than not she'll give me her opinion on what I was wearing or if I got my hair cut or colored (sorry, Mom). Hence, my reasoning that in radio there's a lot less distraction. You must listen.

When I first began at Fox News, I did a fun little "kicker" story with my friend Jane Skinner on her midday news show, *Happening*

Now. It usually followed the weather report, and Jane was the one who came up with the name "The Dean's List." We did it for a few months, but then it went away. Not Jane's fault, it's just in the world of breaking news, unfortunately, the feel-good stories are often the first ones to get cut because of time. But I never forgot those enjoyable moments and how much I loved doing them. So, when Fox Radio asked for ideas, "The Dean's List" was back in business.

I've had such wonderful feedback about these good news stories that it was a natural suggestion when my editor of *Mostly Sunny* asked if there was another possible book in our future together. We met over lunch in the Fox News cafeteria on the third floor (where my friends Selwyn and Curtis greeted us with smiles, kindness, and snacks), and I told Eric all about my favorite Dean's Lists and how I envisioned them becoming the book you see right now. We decided to call it *Make Your Own Sunshine* as a companion to *Mostly Sunny* and keeping with the theme of always trying to look on the bright side.

Of course, it involved quite a bit more work than writing and recording a sixty-second radio hit. I realized I needed to get some help finding these wonderful people and organizing interviews. I remembered a college associate on *Fox & Friends* that I got to know named Isabelle Beyda. She stood out to me because she knew how important it was to find out about everything when it came to television. From producing to writing to being a greenroom assistant, and even to broadcasting the weather. She reminded me of myself when I was just starting out after school, volunteering to do anything and everything while making friends and connections along the way. I've told many young broadcasters that while it's important to do well in school, it sometimes even more beneficial to get to know people in the industry and study what they do. You never know who might be able to help you find your next job.

I reached out to Isabelle and asked if she would be interested in being my assistant for this book. She agreed right away and got to work. Every one of the interviews you've read (with the exceptions of a few I had already arranged before I hired her) was orchestrated by her. I gave her a wish list of who I wanted, and she delivered. If it weren't for Isabelle, I don't think this book would be completed, or as special.

I'd be remiss if I didn't thank the Fox News Radio crew who not only help with my Dean's Lists every day, but also recorded many of these interviews that were then transcribed for the book. To Frank Bruno, Harry Kapsalis, Hank Weinbloom, Jason Austin, George Wright, and John Toldi, thank you for going the extra mile and always with a smile.

I'm so grateful to all my new friends you've read about and who shared their lives. You've read their stories, but I do feel like they've become part of my family. Many of them I've kept in touch with even after our interviews were completed. Several of the chapters involve causes and charities, so at the end of the book, you'll find a list of websites where you can get more information about their organizations.

Thank you to my Fox family, who have truly created a second home for me over seventeen years now. To Suzanne Scott, Lauren Petterson, Dianne Brandi, Gavin Hadden, and Jay Wallace for encouraging my side job as an author in addition to my weather duties.

To the folks at HarperCollins: Eric Nelson who has been not only a wonderful editor but has also been a good friend who has sometimes become a cell phone therapist. To Hannah Long, who helped me stay on deadlines, sifted through photos and edits, and offered suggestions and smart advice.

To Bob Barnett for helping guide my career path and always making time for my phone calls and emails.

My incredible group of girlfriends who I leaned on quite often this last year: Neera Malhotra, Megyn Kelly, Shannon Bream (our little text message prayer group sorority was there when I needed it most),

Meghan McCain, Dervla Geary, and Jen Smrtka. Karen McCracken, Allison Parsons. Vegas will happen at some point. My sparkly dress is waiting.

To Judy Bristol for always being there, listening.

My sister-in-law, Donna, and niece, Danielle. We couldn't have gotten through this past year without you.

To Mickey and Dee, I know you're watching over us.

My mom, Stella, thank you for always being there. Can't wait until we're together again. We love you.

My beautiful boys, Matthew and Theodore. Being your mama is the greatest gift of my life.

To my husband, Sean. The best man I've ever known. Every love story is beautiful, but ours is my favorite.

WEBSITES

- Juvenile Diabetes Research Foundation
  https://www.jdrf.org/

- Garth Callaghan, the Napkin Notes Dad
  https://www.napkinnotesdad.com/

- National Multiple Sclerosis Society
  https://www.nationalmssociety.org/

- Tiny Hero: Helping CDH Families
  https://www.tinyhero.org/

- Malcolm's GoFundMe
  https://www.gofundme.com/f/vsappy-mission-malcolm

- Seth's Rose Rush Facebook page
  https://www.facebook.com/roserushdeliveries/

- Natalie's Nothing but Love Notes
  https://www.nothingbutlovenotes.com/

- St. Baldrick's Foundation
  https://www.stbaldricks.org/

- KiKi's Kindness Project
  https://fundly.com/kikiskindnessproject

- Sir Darius Brown's Facebook page
  https://www.facebook.com/beauxandpaws/

- Information on becoming a foster parent
  https://www.childwelfare.gov/

- Lily's Legacy Senior Dog Sanctuary
  https://www.lilyslegacy.org/

- Ray Pfeifer Foundation
  https://theraypfeiferfoundation.org/

- Pandemic Partners–Bend Facebook page
  https://www.facebook.com/groups/PandemicPartnersBend/

- Tim Tebow Foundation
  https://www.timtebowfoundation.org/

- More Good Today
  https://www.moregood.today/

- Coffee with a Cop
  https://coffeewithacop.com/

- Friends of Officer Conley at JMU Facebook page
  https://www.facebook.com/ConleyAtJmu/

ABOUT THE AUTHOR

JANICE DEAN is the *New York Times* bestselling author of *Mostly Sunny* and the senior meteorologist at Fox News. She serves as the morning meteorologist on *Fox & Friends*. She lives in New York City with her family.